Better Homes and Gardens®

container
gardens

written by Eleanore Lewis

Better Homes and Gardens®
Des Moines, Iowa

Better Homes and Gardens® Books
An imprint of Meredith® Books

Container Gardens
Writer: Eleanore Lewis
Editor and Project Manager: Kate Carter Frederick
Art Director: Lyne Neymeyer
Research Coordinator: Rosemary Kautzky
Project Coordinator: Beth Ann Edwards
Copy Chief: Terri Fredrickson
Managers, Book Production: Pam Kvitne, Marjorie J. Schenkelberg
Contributing Copy Editor: Patrick Davis
Contributing Proofreaders: Mary Duerson, Kathy Roth Eastman
Illustrator: Tom Rosborough
Indexer: Jana Finnegan
Electronic Production Coordinator: Paula Forest
Editorial and Design Assistants: Kaye Chabot, Mary Lee Gavin,
  Karen Schirm

Meredith® Books
Editor in Chief: James D. Blume
Design Director: Matt Strelecki
Managing Editor: Gregory H. Kayko
Executive Garden Editor: Cathy Wilkinson Barash

Director, Retail Sales and Marketing: Terry Unsworth
Director, Sales, Special Markets: Rita McMullen
Director, Sales, Premiums: Michael A. Peterson
Director, Sales, Retail: Tom Wierzbicki
Director, Book Marketing: Brad Elmitt
Director, Operations: George A. Susral
Director, Production: Douglas M. Johnston

Vice President, General Manager: Jamie L. Martin

Better Homes and Gardens® Magazine
Editor in Chief: Jean LemMon
Executive Garden Editor: Mark Kane

Meredith Publishing Group
President, Publishing Group: Stephen M. Lacy
Vice President, Finance and Administration: Max Runciman

Meredith Corporation
Chairman and Chief Executive Officer: William T. Kerr

Chairman of the Executive Committee: E. T. Meredith III

All of us at Better Homes and Gardens® Books are dedicated to providing you with information and ideas to enhance your home and garden. We welcome your comments and suggestions. Write to us at Better Homes and Gardens Books, Garden Editorial Department, 1716 Locust St., Des Moines, IA 50309-3023.

If you would like to purchase any of our books, check wherever quality books are sold. Visit us online at bhgbooks.com.

Cover photograph: Michael Jensen

container
gardens

introduction

portable gardens

Oh, the places they'll go! Containers make gardening so accessible, easy, and variable that they have virtually no drawbacks. Pots let you garden in otherwise impossible places and enliven any setting with their colorful plantings. Set pots in a window box and attach it to a sill or a deck railing. Set a planter on each tread of an entry stairway. Suspend baskets from eaves, overhead beams, and pergolas. Wherever you find a bit of empty space, you have a spot for a container.

The ability to change or rearrange pots and the plants in them in a matter of minutes makes this kind of gardening fun. Don't worry about making a mistake if you follow a few simple guidelines: Combine plants with similar moisture and light requirements, water them frequently during the hottest days of the year, and pay attention to the cold-tolerance (or tenderness) of the plants you choose.

unlimited choices
right: **From small 3-inch plastic pots and petite ceramic urns to large 5- and 10-gallon terra-cotta planters and strawberry jars, the range of sizes and materials available today extends the scope of gardening in containers. Pick a spot for a garden and you'll find a container to match it.**

personal expression

left: Turn an eyesore into an asset using a container. In this case, an old brick pillar becomes a useful pedestal for an outstanding potted rose. Depending on the plants and pots you choose, container gardens also become an expression of your personality. Go formal or informal. Indulge a passion, such as growing herbs. Create the water garden of your dreams without all the work.

high flight

below left: Use trailing plants for their architectural characteristics as well as their bright flowers or foliage. Choose traditional trailers, including petunias and ivy geraniums, or unusual ones, such as these succulents. Hang them where they'll receive adequate light while creating a most dramatic effect.

potted advantages

Compared with in-ground plantings, potted gardens are more temporary, but they also reward spontaneous design and a willingness to change them. Experiment freely with new plants and combinations, knowing you can easily redesign the planters next season. Avoid the chore of amending garden soil, whether it's infertile or drains poorly. Overcome shady locations and brighten dark corners with pots of colorful flowers. Extend the growing season by moving plants indoors over winter. Grow plants you otherwise would not include in your garden. Use limited space more efficiently or break up large areas in your landscape with pots. Keep invasive plants contained so they don't overrun your garden.

container gardens | 7

potpourri of ideas

Containers play several different roles in the landscape. Use them as focal points in a garden. Set up a potted water feature. Employ large, empty urns and amphora-style pots as pieces of art, on their own or grouped with other planted pots.

Fill gaps in a bed with containers you plant with spring- and summer-flowering bulbs for seasonal color; plant perennial- and tropical-bloomers with annuals for all-season color.

In cold-winter areas, care for tender perennials, such as rosemary and salvia

accessorize

right: **A few well-placed accessories reinforce the pattern of pots. Coordinate the materials—terra-cotta, wood, or resin, for example—and the colors of both the accents and the planters.**

'Victoria,' in pots you move indoors for winter. This is much easier than digging them up in fall and better than losing them to a frost. Grow movable gardens of vegetables and herbs right outside the kitchen door, on a deck, or along a walk. Create a boundary around a garden bed with a row of shrubby plants in pots. Or set up a privacy screen between the patio and a neighbor's yard with plants that clamber up tepees and trellises inserted in large planters.

one-of-a-kind designs

The most enticing aspect of gardening in containers is the freedom it gives you to experiment and have fun. However, consider each plant's cultural needs as you combine a variety of plants in one pot or a number of containers in one arrangement. As the set designer, so to speak, of your garden scenes, be bold. Take out, replace, or highlight plants at will. Those plants might not thrive with such treatment in a regular garden.

set a stage
above left: Express your personality and greet visitors by decorating your home's entryway with a potted garden and a collection of delightful ornaments. The setting also adds interest and color.

bright lights
left: Combine bright colors with subdued shades, such as these yellow marigolds and variegated sage, so that each focuses attention on the other.

introduction

pots and plants

The only dilemma you may face when selecting a pot for your garden is choosing from the many materials and finishes available. Consider classic concrete and natural terra-cotta (and lightweight look-alikes for both) as well as rustic wood and contemporary self-watering planters. Synthetic pots last longer and tolerate freezing winters better than most natural materials. Being lightweight, they're also easier to move around.

Soil dries out faster in clay pots than in fiberglass containers, and large planters hold moisture longer than small ones.

Consider style when coordinating your potted plantings. Choose container colors that complement your house, matching them or contrasting them with your outdoor furniture and landscaping materials.

artful design

above: Keep plants in scale with their pots and keep the overall design in proportion to its location. This grouping in front of a picket fence combines delicate chives with lush rosemary and bushy annual geraniums. A few blue pots add color and contrast to the terra-cotta planters.

choices

right: Find a planter to suit your garden's style. Pick one that's plain or decorated with raised designs, shallow or deep. Make sure there's a drainage hole in the bottom of it.

match game

left: Ornamental grasses in improvised planters complement the design of a twig bench. Those same grasses set in classic containers next to a wrought-iron settee would give a totally different impression.

fine focus

below left: Geraniums and million bells top a planter of dusty miller and verbena to create a cheerful focal point for a country garden.

When you choose your plants, remember their mature size. Those tiny 3-inch transplants grow quickly. Even though you plant more closely in a container than you do in the ground, don't overcrowd them. Allow space for root growth and air circulation between the plants.

how to use this book

Your container gardening skills will flourish with the inspiring ideas, tips for success, fundamentals of care, and plant portraits in this book. Every project, whether setting up a window box or making a trough, includes details on materials and skill level, as well as step-by-step directions or diagrams. Start with the gardens themselves–some traditional, others one-of-a-kind. Proceed to places for containers, and then turn to the basics you need to accomplish the designs you dream up. The plant portrait pages contain scores of possible flowers, herbs, vegetables, trees, and shrubs appropriate for potted living–enough to turn your enthusiasm into a passion.

container gardens | **11**

the gardens

window boxes

zones	time	skill
4–10	1–2 hours	easy

you will need

window box: size to match your window ledge; at least 4 in. deep with holes for drainage

lightweight potting mix or soilless mix

plants in 3-in. pots

eye-level beauty

Nothing dresses up a house, from an indoor point of view as well as outside from the street, like window boxes resting on sills or hanging just below. The only tricky part to gardening in window boxes is reaching them to remove spent flowers and to water, but a watering wand attached to a hose helps with the latter chore.

Window gardens span the seasons. To make changes easier, use plants in their pots instead of putting them directly in soil in the box. When using plants already in pots, you can quickly replace spring-blooming bulbs with summer-flowering annuals, followed by low-growing evergreens, such as juniper, for winter color.

adaptable plants

right and below: **This English-style planting will do well in full or partial sun, although the geraniums and periwinkles flower best in exposures with at least six hours of sun daily. If the petunias become too leggy by midsummer, trim them back hard by one-third.**

plants

1 petunia

2 madagascar periwinkle

3 ivy

4 geranium

5 lobelia

1 design Select plants with a variety of growth habits–upright, bushy, and trailing–and with complementary or matching colors. Remember to consider the shapes and colors of foliage as well. Fill the window box three-fourths full with a good potting soil. Mix in water-retentive crystals and a slow-release fertilizer to cut down on watering and feeding during the season; follow label directions. Setting the window box in place before planting makes the job easier.

2 plant Set the plants in their pots on top of the soil; rearrange them until you like the design. Place taller plants toward the back and either the center or the ends. Fill in spaces with bushy plants. Put trailing plants in front to drape over the edge. Use vining plants, such as dwarf morning glory, on the ends; attach small trellises to the box or to the window frame for them to climb on. Unpot plants and set them in the soil at the same depth they were growing before.

3 maintain Water thoroughly after planting. Check soil daily and water to a depth of about 2 to 3 inches when it is dry. To keep the garden neat, pinch off or deadhead spent blooms and remove yellowed or dead leaves. Fertilize monthly if you didn't mix a slow-release fertilizer in with the soil. In midsummer, cut back (by one-third) straggly or nonflowering plants, such as pansies and sweet alyssum, to promote reblooming through the cooler days of autumn.

a change of scene

When planting for seasonal changes, opt for a plastic liner that fits inside the window box instead of just placing potted plants in an empty box. It is easy to lift out the liner to replace plants that have finished blooming. A plastic liner also protects the box from the wearing effects of soil and water, thus extending its life.

A sheet of heavy-duty black plastic achieves the same protection. Staple it to the interior and punch drainage holes in it to match those in the bottom of the box. For a box facing south, use a sheet of plastic foam, which will act as an insulator to reduce the temperature of the soil–especially important in the heat of midsummer.

culinary fragrance

right: Combine herbs, such as thyme, mint, and basil with colorful annuals—violas and nasturtiums here—for double impact. The curly leaves of parsley add contrasting texture to the planting.

lovely in harmony
left: Combine geraniums with plants that have similar flower colors but contrasting foliage shapes and growth habits: trailing blue lobelia and petunias, for example.

swags of green
below: No matter what plants you put in your window box, boost its impact by adding an ivy swag to the design. Make tubes from chicken wire or hardware cloth sized to fit your window box. Stuff the tubes with sphagnum moss and insert rooted ivy cuttings to cover completely. Drape the swags from hooks attached at the ends and middle of the box.

great window box plants

- bacopa
- calendula
- cyclamen
- daisy
- dusty miller
- geranium
- impatiens
- ivy
- lantana
- lobelia
- miniature rose
- nasturtium
- pansy
- parsley
- petunia
- pinks
- plectranthus
- portulaca
- salvia
- scaevola
- swan river daisy
- vinca vine

contrasting colors

right: **Combine contrasting colors, such as yellows and reds, to catch the attention of anyone passing by.**

cottage style

opposite: **Fill a long window box with a profusion of flowers to display nonstop color in an old-fashioned, cottage garden-style design.**

matching hues

right: **Take a cue from the color of your home's trim. Here, blue petunias, salvia, Swan River daisies, and lobelia coordinate with the shutters. Silvery artemisia adds the touch of a contrasting color to the planting. Annual flowering plants are available in so many shades that you're sure to find a few that harmonize with your home's colors. Use foliage plants, such as artemisia and dusty miller, to accent or soften the effect.**

the hang of it

Determine where the bottom of the window box will rest against the house by measuring and marking the box's depth. Use the marks as a guide for installing brace-type supports.

Locate the studs under the window; existing nailheads are a good indication. Secure each brace (metal or wooden) to a stud by screwing the supports into place with 2½-inch deck screws. For extra security, drill several screws through the back of the box and into the studs as well.

For a smooth look, cut triangular wood shims the width of the brackets from rot-resistant wood. Nail them to the clapboard siding to fill the open spaces behind the brackets and each end of the window box.

Ask at your local hardware store for advice on appropriate drill bits and screws for attaching a window box to aluminum siding, brick, stucco, or stone.

container gardens | **19**

wall containers

zones	time	skill
3–10	3–4 hours	moderate

you will need

- wire basket
- sphagnum moss or coconut-husk liner
- potting soil
- all-purpose plant food
- six-packs of flowers: upright and trailing
- heavy-duty hook

wire container

By their very nature, planters made with wire are lighter in weight than those fashioned from wood, ceramic, or terra-cotta. Even so, consider the heaviness of the planted basket when it is wet so that you hang it from a hook sturdy enough to take the weight. Flowers cover the entire visible surface because you plant from the outside through the openings or rungs and not just at the top. Cover the inside of the basket with sphagnum moss or simply line it with a ready-made liner that fits the basket so the soil does not leak out. Water regularly during hot weather.

cheery greeting

right and below: **A pastel mix of pink, yellow, white, and silver greets visitors at the gate. When you plant a wire or moss hanging basket, place trailing flowers near the bottom, where they cascade without concealing other plants.**

plants

1 petunia

2 pansy

3 dusty miller

4 sweet alyssum

1 **line** Hang the basket from a hook so that it stays upright and steady while you plant it. Soak long-fibered sphagnum peat moss in water for a few minutes; squeeze out excess water. Press the moss around the inside of the basket one-third of the way up. Mix all-purpose plant food with the soil. Fill the moss nest with the soil mix.

2 **plant the bottom** Tuck small trailing plants through the wire rungs and into the moss so the roots reach the soil in the center of the basket. Gently firm soil and water well.

Add another layer of moss and soil. Tuck in more plants from the outside.

Continue layering moss, soil, and plants until you reach the top of the planter. Plants near the top can be upright (marigolds, dusty miller), clumping (sedum, sempervivum, sweet alyssum), or trailing (petunias, bacopa).

3 **plant the top** Create a moss nest that reaches just above the top of the basket so it conceals the wire rim. Add soil and upright or bushy plants. Surround the top plants with moss to conserve soil moisture.

Make sure the moss is holding the soil in all around the basket; add more if necessary.

Hang the basket from a hook on a wall, fence, or gate.

Water the planter daily during dry weather. Deadhead spent blooms as necessary.

wall containers

hanging delights

Suspend a garden anywhere–on a wall, fence, or gate–to display appealing colors all season. Because wall planters are usually half-rounds, they fit in smaller spaces. However, planters should be at least 12 inches across and 4 inches deep for good plant growth. Grow just about any annual flower and many perennials and herbs in wall-hung planters.

Grooming is almost as important as the standard maintenance tasks of watering and feeding, which should be done regularly to keep plants healthy. Messy or neglected containers become eyesores. Take a few mintues each day to groom your potted plants: Deadhead spent flowers, remove yellowed leaves, cut back straggly plants, and carefully pull out plants past their prime.

create a wall pattern

right: Arrange containers of individual plants, such as bushy geraniums, on a wall in a stepped pattern. It's a memorable effect. Smaller pots lose moisture more quickly than large planters. Clay or terra-cotta containers absorb soil moisture, so check plantings daily for dryness. Water more than once a day, if necessary.

mixed plantings

below: For wire planters, purchase annuals in six-packs. Their small root balls fit easily through the openings when you plant them.

match-up

left: Coordinate the material of your planter with the wall on which you hang it for a neat, unobtrusive design. Such an arrangement highlights the flowering plants such as pansies, geraniums, petunias, and lobelia, instead of the planter, as shown by this wooden box mounted on natural wood siding.

rustic scene

below left: Water leaking out of moss-lined wire baskets (as well as clay or terra-cotta planters) can harm porous surfaces, such as wood, underneath. Apply a water sealant to the surface before you mount the basket.

prevent a problem

below right: For instant color, start with plants in bloom. Select seedlings to provide a longer show that grows gradually to fill the planter.

hanging baskets

zones	time	skill
3–11	1 hour	easy

you will need

- wire basket
- liner of sphagnum moss or coconut husk
- lightweight or soilless potting mix
- slow-release fertilizer
- water-saving polymer crystals
- various plants
- heavy-duty hook or swivel hook
- chains for hanging

wire basket

Hanging baskets lend a particularly festive air to a porch, a deck, or an entryway if you suspend more than one from the roof or eaves. (Remember to hang them higher than the heights–and heads–of your friends.) Plant individual containers with one type of flower, such as geraniums or impatiens, for the easiest scheme. Make monochromatic arrangements, with one color in each pot or shades of the same color in a number of pots. Group baskets for a dramatic effect. Create abundant gardens by mixing different flower and foliage types.

mixed colors and shapes

right and below: **This basket looks great on a table or pedestal. The clustered white and multicolored flowers of candytuft and lantana form the perfect base for the red salvia.**

plants

1 candytuft
2 lantana
3 salvia

1 line Line your wire-form hanging basket with a water-absorbent material such as sphagnum moss or coconut-husk fiber. Cut the latter to fit and make one or more slits from the edge to the center to help you set the liner snugly in the basket. If you prefer, simply purchase a ready-made liner designed to fit the basket you choose.

Soak the liner in water overnight to soften and moisten it so it will be easier to handle and shape to fit the basket.

2 fill Use a soilless or lightweight potting mix to fill the lined basket; moisten the mix before use. To cut down on watering and feeding during the season, add a slow-release fertilizer and water-saving polymer crystals to the mix when you fill the basket.

Remember that regular garden and potting soils tend to be heavy when wet. Soilless mixes remain lighter when wet—an important consideration when hanging a container from a hook.

3 plant Plant a variety of flowering and vining plants. Hanging baskets are often viewed from below, so set trailing plants, such as vinca, petunias, nasturtiums, or ivy-leaf geraniums, along the rim and upright plants toward the center.

Water the planter thoroughly when you have finished and let it drain before hanging.

The hook you use for suspending the basket should be designed for heavy weight.

hanging baskets

summertime plants

right: In lightly shaded locations, combine annuals, such as impatiens and scented geraniums, with plants that spend cold winters indoors, such as spider plants, swedish ivy, and ivy. At the end of the outdoor growing season, gently pull out and discard the annuals and bring the tender plants back indoors until the following summer.

water wise

below: If the container you want to use doesn't have a drainage hole and you don't want to drill one, take extra precautions. With no way to drain, excess water builds up in soil, eventually killing the plants due to lack of oxygen to their roots or rot at the crown. Place an inch of gravel in the bottom of the pot at planting time. Check soil moisture before watering by poking your finger at least an inch into the soil. Water only when the soil feels thoroughly dry and don't drench it.

tower of power

above: Turn suspended plants into pillars of greenery and flowers. Fill hanging baskets with trailing plants. As they mature, their cascading stems will create veils of cool colors.

scented pleasure

left: Hang pots of scented plants from a bracket installed near a door or a window. You'll enjoy the fragrance every time you pass by. Freesia *(shown)*, jasmine, petunias, heliotrope, and small-flowered daffodils provide lovely colors as well as scent.

classic containers

zones	time	skill
3–11	weekend	moderate

you will need

container, as desired

flat latex paint: black and one contrasting color

paintbrush

liquid glaze

rags

clear sealant spray

faux verdigris

Using this simple technique of painting and dabbing, you'll give containers an aged, weathered look. All it takes is two coats of contrasting colors.

weathered look

right and below:
Simulate the real verdigris finish on metal pots that results from years of exposure to the elements.

plants

1 geranium

2 petunia

3 gerbera daisy

4 dusty miller

1 base coat Antique any surface, including terra-cotta, plastic, and metal. The technique looks best on pieces with cracks, crevices, and details. Do a trial run on the bottom of the pot so any mistakes you make won't show on the finished product.

Begin by painting a base coat with one color of latex paint. Flat black latex paint, used here, gives a terra-cotta pot the look of a bronze urn with a verdigris finish. Allow the base coat to dry completely.

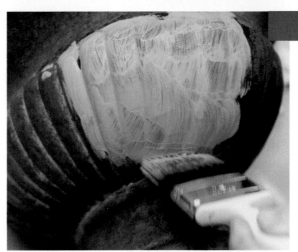

2 top coat Prepare the top coat by mixing a latex glaze liquid with a second color of latex paint. Use a ratio of about one part glaze to four parts paint. Apply the top coat (at left, a slightly gaudy aqua).

Latex paint dries fast, so paint only a small area at a time (about the size of a baseball card). Leave irregular edges, and then blend them as you continue to paint, using the antiquing technique described below.

3 antiquing Immediately after you apply a section of top coat, wad up a rag and blot or dab the paint gently. Soften the edges first, then go over the middle. Move and remove the top coat until you achieve a look that you like.

When you have covered the entire surface, let the paint dry completely. Seal with three coats of clear sealant spray; allow the sealant to dry completely between the coats.

what's in a classic

Modern classic containers replicate designs from country and royal estates in 18th- and 19th-century Europe, and they add a finished look to our typically smaller gardens. Whether vaselike urns or square, rectangular, or round planters, classic containers share a simplicity and elegance of form that never go out of style. Often large, with decorative embellishments circling the rim or base, these planters usually appear in subtle, stony colors. They harmonize easily with most settings as well as with the plants they hold. Modern, resin, and fiberglass versions of stone and concrete classics offer lightweight portability. Placed on a pedestal, they're classic.

fleur-de-lis squared

above right: Use a single planter as the focal point of a patio; use pairs of planters to mark the entrance to a garden or house.

fine fakery

right: Gone are the days of dragging heavy concrete containers around now that lightweight and weatherproof composition pots are available. This terracotta look-alike holds sweet potato vine, variegated sage, coleus, dusty miller, and dwarf arborvitae.

urned rewards

above: The scalloped leaves of succulents, such as these echeveria, mirror the design etched into the sides of this shallow antique planter. Many other plants accomplish a similar effect: With their grasslike foliage, carex, daylilies, and irises would resemble the lines on a ridged container, for example.

classic surprise

left: When you place a topiary in a pot, aim for the emphasis to be on the plant, not the pot. Choose a container with a simple design in a subdued color, so it plays a supporting role and doesn't compete with the plant or overshadow it. Be a bit playful, however, if you want—here, the red-ribbon bow adds color while repeating the pot's ribbon design.

container gardens | **31**

classic containers

succulent scene

right: A traditional combination of sedum and sempervivum dresses up the corner of a patio. Succulents such as these offer intriguing textures and colors and ask for very little in return. Infrequent watering and a location that receives morning sun and afternoon shade are especially crucial in hot climates.

ageless simplicity

below left: Slow-growing boxwood is a time-honored plant for containers. It epitomizes the classic practice of using only one, striking plant in a pot. Mulch the bare soil surrounding it or plant an unobtrusive living groundcover, such as ivy. Prune boxwood yearly to retain its shape.

today's classic

below right: Hardy ornamental grasses such as this fountain grass give classic concrete urns and Versailles-style planters an updated look. Grasses are low maintenance and appropriate in any garden design, whether modern or traditional.

beyond tradition

above: Standard, or tree-form, plants, such as this shrub rose, fit best in formal settings. Encircle them with a jumble of less formal plants, however, and they will harmonize beautifully with a country-style garden. Choose herbs—fragrant, useful, and usually informal in their growth habits—for ideal planting partners.

special show-off

left: Boldly display one of your favorite containers by *not* planting in it. The effect is stunning and classic. Accompany it with a lushly planted, more ordinary pot, such as this one filled with coleus, nasturtiums, bacopa, and morning glory climbing a plant support.

container gardens | **33**

topiaries

zones	time	skill
3–10	1 hour	moderate

you will need

10–12-in. decorative pot

potting soil

topiary form

four 16-in.-long bamboo stakes (optional)

green florist's wire (any gauge)

ivy plants (1–2 large hanging baskets or 4–5 small plants)

green cloth-covered wire (optional)

live moss

U-shape florist pins

classic form

The art of topiary–or training vines, shrubs, trees, and other slow-growing plants into various shapes–dates back to formal Roman gardens in the first century A.D. Today, these plant sculptures pop up everywhere: indoors and in small, informal gardens, as well as on patios and decks. Make your topiaries easily using traditional plants, such as ivy and yew, and readily available forms, from spirals and globes to animal shapes, such as rabbits and bears. Start with unusual plants (*see list below*), if you feel more daring. Start with simple forms and progress to more complex ones as you build confidence.

easy maintenance

right: **Care for a topiary the same way you would any potted plant: watering as needed, fertilizing periodically, and trimming to shape occasionally.**

great plants for topiaries

- boxwood
- creeping fig
- dwarf japanese holly
- fuchsia
- ivy
- juniper
- lavender
- privet
- rosemary
- santolina
- scented-leaf geranium
- yew

1 place form Fill a container with rich potting soil and tamp down. Center a topiary form in the pot and press it into the soil. The base of the form should be level with the soil surface and sit securely in place.

2 anchor form For a form with a central spine, use bamboo stakes to anchor it in the soil. Insert four stakes closely around the spine and push them partway into the soil. Then hold the stakes against the spine and wire them to the form using florist's wire.

3 plant Use ivy or other plants with at least one long trailing stem. Push aside enough soil in the pot to make room for each plant's root ball. Plant ivy, leaving space for growth between plants. Cover root balls with soil. Continue planting until you fill the pot.

4 wind Carefully wind long ivy trailers around the form, securing with cloth-covered wire if necessary. Cover soil and base of form with moss; secure with florist's pins. Water. As ivy grows, continue to wind stems. Maintain shape by clipping bushy growth.

container gardens | **35**

topiaries

poodle shapes

right: Plump spheres of ivy provide classic accents next to doorways and garden entrances. To maintain plants in the shape you desire, prune any errant growth.

not-so-standard fare

below: Also known as a tree-form, a standard is impressive to look at but not difficult to achieve. Plants with sturdy or woody main stems, such as rosemary, lavender, scented geraniums, and boxwood, make good candidates for this form of topiary. Insert a stake beside the stem for support while the stem grows to the height you want; remove lower side shoots when the height has been reached.

petite herbal forest

above left: Turn edible and ornamental herbs into pretty miniature standards that grow as well indoors on a sunny windowsill as they do outdoors in the garden. Clip new growth frequently to retain the shape. Start with larger plants for more instant gratification.

welcoming wreath

above right: Lavender grows well as a spiral and makes an excellent candidate for wreaths, too. Purchase the circular form or make one of your own by bending a wire coat hanger into a circle. Straighten the hanger's hook and poke it into the pot of soil.

cascades of flowers

left: Fuchsia makes a wonderful standard because the form brings the numerous pendant flowers to eye level. Bring container-grown standards indoors for winter. They don't survive outdoors year-round in colder zones. Return them to the garden come spring.

shallow bowls

zones	time	skill
3–10	1 hour	easy

you will need

wide, shallow
terra-cotta container

soilless potting mix
made of peat moss
and vermiculite

piece of window
screening

assorted perennials,
ornamental
vegetables

temporary color

No matter what the
season, containers
bursting with color
help to brighten dull
spots, accent a patio or
deck, or highlight your
favorite flowers. All it
takes is a bit of
advance planning. By
observing when certain
plants peak in
performance and acknowledging when they have
passed their prime, you will recognize when it's
time to remove them from the container and
replace them. If they are perennials, resettle them
in a garden bed.

When you go to the garden center, visualize
how the plants will look together, even if you don't
have the container with you. Lay out your design
ideas in your shopping basket or wagon.

color now

right and below: **Start with mature plants to
create containers with immediate impact.
For longer bloom time, of course, select
younger plants.**

plants

1 *aster novi-belgii*
  'crimson brocade'

2 chrysanthemum

3 sedum

4 variegated ivy

5 korean rock fern

6 ornamental cabbage

1 **select a pot** Wide, shallow containers make attractive homes for an abundance of plants. Starting with mature plants means this is a temporary planting, and you don't need to be concerned about the long-term fertility of the soil. A lightweight, soilless mix of peat moss and vermiculite offers an adequate support for the plants. If you prefer, use garden soil or a packaged potting mix. Before adding soil, place a piece of window screening over the drainage holes to keep them from clogging.

2 **pack them in** For an instant show of color, set plants close together. Pay attention to colors and textures; they should complement one another. Set a plant with frilly leaves next to one with very fine leaves. Offset these with bolder leaves, such as those of chrysanthemums, and lighter green foliage, like that of sedums.

Scoop a depression in the mix and set the plants in at the same depth as they were growing in their nursery pots. Water the finished planting well. Keep the soil mix evenly moist.

spring show
above: Primroses, interplanted with ferns, bring bright colors to semishaded areas in late spring. Transplant them to a garden bed when they finish blooming.

fleeting accent
above right: Some plants produce showier foliage than flowers, while blooms fade quickly on other plants, so pay attention to foliage color and shape when shopping for your plants.

summery shades
right: Begonias, coleus, and alternanthera provide a bonanza of summer color in shady spots. To maintain a neat appearance, pinch off the blooms of coleus as they begin to grow.

edible surprise

left: Combine edible flowers, such as pansies, with colorful red-leaf lettuce for a garden that's equally at home in light shade and sunshine.

seaworthy

below left: Abalone shells make unusual containers for tiny plants, such as these succulents.

ready for spring

below right: Plant tulips in fall for a mid- to late-spring show. Chill potted tulips over winter. Protect them from freezing in a garage or unheated basement. Tuck pansies among the bulbs in the spring.

troughs

zones	time	skill
4–10	half-day	experienced

you will need

- wheelbarrow, hoe
- 6 quarts #20 sand
- 12 quarts peat moss
- 6 quarts cement
- 1½ cups fiber mesh
- garden hose
- mold container: approx. 13×17×8 in.
- large plastic bags or sheets of plastic
- string
- 3-ft.-square board
- rubber gloves
- two 6-in. lengths PVC pipe
- trowel
- wire brush
- muriatic acid

cozy home

Troughs originally were no more than natural depressions in large rocks and stones. Savvy European plant collectors turned these hollows into protected pockets for the plants they found in their wanderings. They also carved sink-size troughs out of stone.

Imitate ancient troughs, weathered and covered with lichen or moss, by mixing peat moss and concrete and shaping a trough in a plastic mold. The result looks and feels like stone but costs less. Make troughs in a garage or basement where you won't damage the floor or expose your trough to the weather while it cures.

To get lichen or moss to grow on your trough, paint it with buttermilk or yogurt after it has

great plants for troughs

- alyssum
- armeria
- candytuft
- draba
- dwarf columbine
- moss phlox
- mosses
- pieris
- primrose
- rock cress
- saxifrage
- sedums
- thyme
- verbena

cured. Alternatively, paint the trough with latex paint, using a neutral color that blends with other materials in the yard. Before you fill the trough with soil, place a piece of old window screen over each of the drainage holes.

Plants for the trough should have similar requirements for type of soil, sunlight, moisture, and nutrients. Woodland plants, for example, do best in a soil mix that contains extra leaf mold to lighten it. Alkaline-loving alpine plants need a few lime chips added to raise the pH.

culture

Water thoroughly after planting and regularly through the season. Fertilize the garden with a water-soluble food diluted to half the strength recommended on the label.

In Zones 3-8, move the trough garden into a protected location for winter; bring troughs filled with tender plants indoors.

look closely

left and below: Trough gardens invite a closer look, during which you'll appreciate the varied shapes, textures, and colors of the plant gems that might otherwise be lost in a garden bed.

plants

1 sedum
2 creeping thyme
3 armeria
4 sweet box
5 campanula
6 verbena
7 salvia
8 dwarf cyclamen
9 bacopa

1   **mix** The amounts of materials listed on the previous page result in a trough that measures approximately 13×17×8 inches. Mix the sand and peat moss in a wheelbarrow, using a hoe to blend them together. Add the concrete; mix. Add the fiber mesh. When you have blended all the materials, add water from a hose, a little at a time. Stir after each addition until the mixture sticks together and resembles thick cooked oatmeal.

2   **mold preparation** Select a large container to use as a mold, such as a plastic garden pot, plastic foam container, or oversize bowl. Wrap it in a large plastic bag or sheet of plastic, covering the entire surface.

Form the trough on either the inside or outside of the mold. Form the trough on the inside of the container by placing the plastic on the inside of it. If you are forming the trough on the outside, put the plastic on the outside. Do not worry about wrinkles; they will create texture in the finished piece. Hold the plastic in place by tying a string around the container. Set the container on a vinyl- or plastic-covered board so you can turn the board and work on all sides of the container.

3   **mold inside** To form the trough on the inside of the mold, firmly press the mixture into the bottom of the covered container, building it up at least 3 inches thick. Place two pieces of PVC pipe upright in the bottom to create drainage holes.

Work up the sides, forming walls that are even in width and firmly packed. Smooth the surface with a trowel.

mold outside To form the trough on **4** the outside of the mold, turn the container upside down and press the mixture around the sides and bottom. Build the walls and bottom at least 3 inches thick. Smooth with a trowel. Place the two PVC pipes upright in the bottom to form drainage holes.

cure and finish Cover the trough **5** loosely with plastic or vinyl and place it in the shade to dry slowly. In hot weather, mist the trough occasionally to keep it from drying too quickly and cracking.

The trough should be dry to the touch in about a week, depending on the dampness of the weather, but it should be soft enough to texture the surface.

Carefully remove the mold. With a wire brush, work the surface to scrape away loose cement and to create ridges or designs.

Place the trough in the shade and let it cure for a month.

Before planting the trough, neutralize the cement by soaking it in a mixture of four parts water to one part muriatic acid. Let dry.

Move the trough to a permanent location. Fill with a soil mix appropriate for the kind of plants you want to grow. After planting, mulch the soil with a quarter-inch covering of granite chips, limestone, or pea gravel.

strawberry jars

zones	time	skill
3–11	1 hour	easy

you will need

- strawberry jar
- potting soil
- 2¼-in.-wide PVC pipe, long enough to reach the top of the jar (optional)
- drill
- plants, enough to fill the number of pockets in the jar

space-wise

Originally, strawberry jars or pots were used only for raising strawberries, which send out runners to produce new plants. The pot's design suits the plants perfectly, with pockets cut into it here and there that hold just enough soil to support a plant. Tucking each plantlet (still attached to a runner) into one of the pockets yields a decorative and productive small-space garden.

Strawberry jars have come a long way over the years. These versatile planters, ideal for patios and decks, now hold all kinds of plants, from flowers and herbs to cacti and succulents.

water smart

right: **An alternative watering method ensures that water reaches all levels of tall jars. Drill holes in a length of 2¼-inch-diameter PVC pipe at 3- to 4-inch intervals. Fill the jar with soil and insert the pipe in the center. Pour water into the pipe; it will seep down and out.**

great plants for strawberry jars

- geranium
- hen and chicks
- ivy
- lettuces
- lobelia
- pansy
- parsley
- petunia
- pinks
- portulaca
- rosemary
- sedum
- strawberry
- sweet alyssum
- thyme

1 soil Any packaged potting soil will do. You have two choices in how you plant a strawberry jar: as you fill it with soil or after you have put soil in all the way to within about 2 inches of the top. For the first method, fill the jar to the lowest pocket and firm the soil to eliminate air spaces, but don't pack it down too tightly. For the second method, firm the soil as you fill the jar to the top, making sure the soil goes into the pockets as well as the center of the planter.

2 plants Starting with the lowest pocket, make a hole in the soil and slip the plant's root ball into the pocket, spreading the roots toward the interior of the jar. For the first method. add more soil until you reach the next pocket level, firming it as you fill. For the second method, the technique for planting is the same except that you won't be able to reach down into the jar to spread the plant's roots out. You will need to work them into the soil from the outside.

3 top and care Save the most upright plants for the open top; set the root ball at the same level it was growing in its nursery pot. Water the container well. Tuck back in any soil that washes out of the pockets. Leakage may occur until the plants and their roots resume growing. Water and fertilize frequently. To ensure that all the plants get an equal share of sun, rotate the jar one-quarter turn every few days.

strawberry jars

lush plantings

The simplest plantings of cacti, edibles, herbs, or tried-and-true annuals make the best choices for a garden in a strawberry jar. Part of the appeal of such a garden is the container itself, so don't completely hide it. Let trailing plants spill their flowers over the outside of the jar. Put bushier, upright plants at the top, spaced close together, to add height and impact. Think about combining edibles, such as herbs and leaf lettuces, in some of the pockets along with your flowering annuals.

Use a strawberry jar to hold a collection of your favorite plants, especially diminutive varieties that otherwise might be lost in the average garden setting.

garden in a jar
right: **With their low moisture requirements, cacti and succulents survive well in the limited pocket spaces. Panda plant and aeonium have room to spread at the top.**

herbal delight

left: Many herbs that benefit from dry conditions flourish in a jar with occasional supplemental watering. Try creeping types of herbs, including thyme and rosemary, as well as upright varieties, such as sage, marjoram, basil, parsley, and catmint. Keep rampant herbs, such as mint, within bounds by harvesting sprigs of the leafy stems regularly for cooking.

patio decor

below left: Pocket plantings create a decorative accent on a patio. Filled with impatiens, geraniums, and begonias, the pots bloom from early summer until the first frost in fall. Ivy-leaf geraniums offer great choices for the middle to lower pockets of the jar, where their trailing-but-sturdy stems create a waterfall of flowers. Use zonal geraniums, which have a more upright growth habit, in the upper pockets or top space.

wooden boxes

zones	time	skill
4–9	1–2 hours	easy

you will need

- wooden box: any length and width; at least 8 in. deep
- potting soil
- sand (optional)
- various herbs: basil, chives, cilantro, sage, dill, thyme

fragrant planting

Enjoy a combination of fragrant herbs and annuals in a rustic wooden box, that you make or buy ready-made. Ensure drainage by drilling holes in the bottom.

color touches

right and below: **For additional color, include fragrant, low-growing flowers such as sweet alyssum and marigolds.**

plants

1. yarrow
2. dill
3. sage
4. basil
5. thyme
6. chives
7. cilantro
8. sweet alyssum
9. marigold

1 select plants For the best, most attractive design, choose plants with complementary colors, shapes, and textures. Most herbs have the same basic soil needs (fertile but not too moist), so you can concentrate on creating pretty combinations.

2 fill Fill a box with a good potting soil. (You can use garden soil, but it may contain weed seeds or insects.) If desired, mix a little sand into the soil to improve drainage, because herbs do not grow well in wet soil.

3 plant Remove plants from their nursery pots and transplant them into the box, placing taller herbs toward the back. You don't need to space the plants the way you would in the ground; instead, snuggle them together.

4 finish Set low-growing plants, such as thyme and sweet alyssum, at the front of the planter, where they'll tumble over the sides. Water the soil thoroughly and place the planter where it will receive full sun for at least 6 hours daily.

wooden boxes

zones	time	skill
3–11	1–2 days	moderate

you will need

- ¾-in. exterior-grade plywood (box)
- 2×2s (posts)
- 1×2s (trim and cap)
- four 2-in. wooden ball finials
- galvanized screws or nails
- drill with ¾-in. bit
- circular saw

classic style

A simple wooden cube forms the basis for many different planter styles. Add posts and finials for a classic look. Attach a trellis to a 6-foot-long, plain box to create a decorative privacy screen next to the patio. Turn old crates and baskets into containers for edibles in a matter of minutes. The possibilities are limited only by your imagination and, in some cases, by your do-it-yourself skills. When building wooden containers, start with cedar or another weather-resistant lumber. Always make drainage holes in any wooden container.

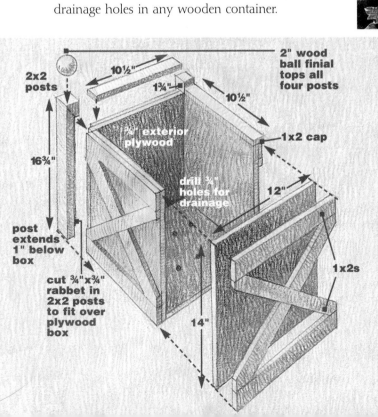

- 2x2 posts
- 10½"
- 1¾"
- 10½"
- 2" wood ball finial tops all four posts
- ¾" exterior plywood
- 1x2 cap
- 16¾"
- drill ¾" holes for drainage
- 12"
- post extends 1" below box
- cut ¾"x¾" rabbet in 2x2 posts to fit over plywood box
- 14"
- 1x2s

greens envy
above left: Plant a garden of lettuces and greens in wooden crates that started life with a different purpose: holding bulbs, strawberries, and other fruits, such as peaches.

country accent
above right: The simplicity of pansies pairs beautifully with the casual look of wood. Mix flower colors for a lovely display.

privacy planter
left: Attach a lattice screen to the back of a planter. It will provide privacy as well as a handsome support for climbing plants, if desired.

tire planter

you will need

- automobile tire with rim attached
- chalk
- finely serrated, sharp knife
- work gloves
- tin snips or pruner
- latex paint and paintbrush
- potting soil
- plants, as desired

recycled art

The idea of using a tire as a planter is decades old, but the design here gives it a new spin and turns it into a form of yard art. Tires are a little bulky and awkward to work with, but they make very long-lasting planters. Paint the tire a light color. Dark colors, such as the tire's original black, tend to absorb heat from summer sun, which can harm the plants. If you want to skip the paint job, use trailing plants around the rim of the tire to cover most of its surface or use spreading or bushy plants in the ground around the permimeter.

unusual container

right and below: **Tire planters make excellent focal points in herb gardens, cornerstones on patios, or simple circular beds in the middle of a small patch of lawn.**

plants

1. verbena
2. japanese blood grass
3. parrot's beak
4. moneywort 'aurea'
5. sweet alyssum
6. zinnia

1 cut pattern Use a standard automobile tire still attached to a rim for easiest handling. Truck and tractor tires, though spacious, prove harder to handle. Avoid radial tires because they're too difficult to maneuver and to cut. Trace a scallop pattern with chalk around the sidewall of the tire before you begin cutting. Make the first and last scallops meet evenly at the beginning and the end. Using a strong, sharp knife with a serrated blade, carefully cut the pattern, as shown.

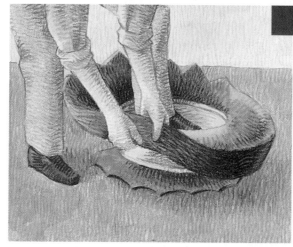

2 inside out Turn the tire over. With the cut side down, slide your gloved hands into the opening you cut in Step 1. Place a foot firmly on the rim of the tire and–with one hand pulling and the other pushing–start to turn the tire inside out. This takes some brute force and perhaps two people, depending on your strength. Continue pulling and pushing all around the tire until you have the inside facing out.

3 trim and plant Point the top edge up. Use tin snips or a pruner to trim the scalloped edge as you like.

Set the tire where you want it to be when planted. (You won't want to move it.) Paint it any color you wish and let dry completely.

Fill with an enriched potting mix. Plant herbs, annuals, dwarf ornamental grasses, miniature roses, or a combination of any of those.

wooden barrels

rustic classic

Planting a wooden whiskey barrel, or half-barrel, as it is often called, couldn't be easier. Line the tub, if you like, with a black plastic trash bag to extend the life of the barrel. Punch drainage holes in the bottom to correspond with those you drill in the barrel. Roll the sides of the bag below the rim after you fill the barrel with a premoistened potting mix. Blend in a slow-acting fertilizer so you won't need to feed the plants for at least a couple of months.

Barrels and edibles go together well. The rustic appearance of the barrel offers a subdued background for the plants, and the roomy interior provides plenty of space for deep root growth. Barrels accommodate almost any vegetable or herb.

growing up

right: Trellises attach easily to barrels, where they provide vertical support for vining crops, such as cucumbers and squash.

salsa garden

left: Turn a few plants, including tomato, hot pepper, tomatillo, and cilantro, into a decorative and potentially delicious salsa garden. Tie the tops of four 1×2s together with twine or wire to make a colorful tepee and top it with an aluminum ornament. Jazz up the barrel and tepee using exterior latex paints in an assortment of bright hues. Guide the tomato and tomatillo vines in and around the tepee as they grow.

take control

below: To control gregarious plants with a tendency to spread, such as sage and mint, plant them in a barrel or a wooden bucket. Enjoy this focal point by adding it to an herb garden, a perennial bed, or a broad patch of lawn.

birdhouse planter

zones	time	skill
4–9	4–5 hours	moderate

you will need

- birdhouse, as desired
- 15–20 cedar or asphalt shingles
- 3d finishing nails
- 2½-in.-long flathead nails
- sheet moss
- spanish moss
- U-shape florist's picks
- four 6-packs of plants
- 30 plants in 6-packs and 3-in. pots

for birds and you

Besides offering resting spots for feathered friends, birdhouses also present a delightful accent in the garden if you imagine their planting possibilities. With the addition of a custom roof and some moss, you'll create a place where small plants can spread their roots. Set the planted birdhouse in partial shade to protect it from drying effects of direct sun. Remove spent flowers to keep plants producing new blooms. Replace plants every year; transplant hardy ivies and chrysanthemums to the garden.

flower sanctuary

right and below: **An ordinary birdhouse becomes extraordinary when the roof overflows with flowers. A 2-inch-deep base provides just enough space to accommodate a few more plants.**

plants

1. chrysanthemum
2. miniature rose
3. variegated ivy
4. impatiens
5. fern

1 roof Raise the birdhouse on the 2-inch tray by nailing it to a 2×4 support. Nail the 2×4 bottom to the tray. Cover the original roof with cedar or asphalt shingles by overlapping and attaching them using finishing nails. Allow an overhang on the sides. Overlap the shingles at the roof's apex. If you use cedar shingles, drill pilot holes before nailing to prevent splitting the shingles. Hammer 2½-inch nails 2 inches apart in staggered rows, jutting up 1 inch, for attaching moss.

2 moss Soak sheet moss in water until it is thoroughly wet; wring out most of the water. Attach the moss to the roof by slipping it over and between the nails.

Immerse potted plants in a bucket of water mixed with a liquid fertilizer. A starter fertilizer that contains B vitamins helps plants resist transplant shock. Follow the package directions for the correct amount.

3 plant Remove plants from their pots and push the root ball of each onto one of the nails on the roof. Cover the bare soil with wet moss using florist picks. Plant the base of the birdhouse, placing plants along the edge. Tuck pieces of Spanish moss between the plantings for a decorative finish.

Water plants gently every day or two–daily in hot, dry weather. Feed every other week with a water-soluble fertilizer.

one-of-a-kind containers

garden art

Gardening, whether in the ground or in containers, should be fun. Finding unusual accent pieces to decorate your garden beds and borders adds to the sometimes childlike wonder of growing plants. Granted, some garden art is definitely frivolous, but finding a new use for an old, derelict object is not. It goes hand in hand with a gardener's desire to waste nothing.

look around

A vintage object, such as the '60s-era bike here, takes on a new purpose if you use a little imaginaton.

plants on the go

right: **Turn an old, battered bike into an eye-catching garden accent. Place upright and trailing plants in front and rear baskets. First line the baskets with sphagnum moss; then fill with a good potting mix or garden soil. For extra whimsy, set a topiary rabbit on the rear fender or the seat.**

The wire baskets on the bike hold plants perfectly if you line them with sphagnum moss.

Bikes also make great trellises for climbing plants–as do outgrown swing sets; just place potted plants on the seats and train the vines up the chains and along the crossbars.

have fun

Think about your old tools that no longer work right or are too rusted to fix. A tripod of hoe, shovel, and rake (bound together at the top and stuck in a large planter) supports pole beans or morning glories. For a movable garden, plant directly in a wood or metal wagon or wheelbarrow, or use either to hold pots.

Kids' toys, the ubiquitous leaky boots, the odd piece of furniture (chair or tv cabinet), sink, or even a bathtub represent plantable possibilities for garden art. Pieces of broken statuary, especially hollow heads or torsos, make great planters, too.

Don't be too serious, but don't overdo either: Whimsy has to have a light touch to be effective; otherwise, it can turn into something grotesque and spoil your garden design.

plants

1 begonia

2 madagascar periwinkle

3 plectranthus

4 pentas

5 ivy

have a seat

right: Take an old, battered chair and train any large-leaf vining plant, such as this ivy, up and over the seat, back, and down the legs. Simply place the potted plant on the seat. Lacking a sturdy seat, set the pot in the frame or fashion a seat from a piece of plywood. Guide the stems to get them to conform to the shape of the chair. Morning glory, black-eyed Susan vine, or cup-and-saucer vine would cover equally well and add flowers to the design.

slipper art

above left: Stuff the open metal frame of a fancy shoe with sphagnum moss and plant green moss to cover it. Moss from your yard grows best if you place the shoe in the same exposure as the moss was growing originally and keep it moist.

any old pot

above right: Give old crates, buckets, and work shoes new life by filling them with potting soil and plants. Moss rose, mimulus, impatiens, geraniums, or sedum will bloom happily all season.

heads up

left: Placed amid regular containers, an unusual one causes visitors to turn their heads.

vroom!

right: A weathered stone rabbit gets a ride on the seat of this child's toy racer. The rabbit appears to be holding a bunch of dusty miller that is planted in a pot of soil where the driver's seat of the car used to be. Turn any toy a child has outgrown—fire truck, doll carriage, or building blocks—into a planter as long as it is intact enough to hold soil or a pot or two.

water wonders

right: Turn a galvanized water trough into the unexpected base for a classic wall fountain. Cluster a simple collection of artful containers around it— with and without plants—and voilà! You quickly complete a garden scene that's both interesting and delightful.

herbal appeal

above: Turn vintage finds from flea markets and garage sales into herb planters. Both green and silver herbs, including basil, thyme, and flat- and curly-leaf parsley, make perfect foils for these colorful olive oil tins. Drill holes in the bottom of the tins for drainage. Set the tins in a location protected from the midday sun because metal heats up quickly, and you don't want to cook your herbs until you harvest them.

novel applications

left: Save precious garden tools, such as these galvanized watering cans, by turning them into unique planters when they no longer serve their original function after years of use and battering. The bright rosy pink geraniums and deep blue petunias here contrast beautifully with the patina of the cans.

quirky drama

right: Turn your favorite collectible, from travels or hobbies, into a stunning centerpiece for the garden or patio. Fill the container with a dramatic plant, such as this phormium, to make a memorable focal point.

light touches

below: Terra-cotta fowl hold sedum and sempervivum—especially appropriate because sempervivum is otherwise known as hen and chicks.

glimpse of the past

above left: Improvise a plant nook with a discarded oven rack and a collection of old teakettles and baking tins. Use seasonal plants, such as petunias, that produce colorful blooms all summer and last until the first fall frosts.

basil in a bath

above right: When is a window box not a window box? When it's a self-watering planter disguised as a kitchen garden, such as this one, packed full of herbs and kept handy on the patio or the deck. A reservoir in the bottom holds the water. Pot feet raise the planter off the ground and facilitate air circulation, which in turn supports plant health and prevents staining on the patio or the deck.

up in smoke

left: Bottomless chimney flue tiles offer ideal drainage for plants. Available in a variety of sizes, they form stepped groupings and also look good in combination with other standard terra-cotta or wooden planters.

container gardens | **67**

potted water garden

zones	time	skill
3–10	weekend	moderate

you will need

- 22×32-in. ceramic pot
- 23-in. metal manger basket
- sheet plastic
- 23-in. coconut husk basket liner
- 50-quart bag potting mix
- potted plants, as desired
- three 48-in. bamboo stakes
- small water pump
- 24-in. bamboo water spout

making music

The sound of water trickling or pouring from a fountain or a spout masks obtrusive noises and creates natural, soothing music. Place a simple, Asian-style bamboo spout in a pot to bring that melody up close in your garden. Set tropical or subtropical plants in a container at the edge of the water garden. Or use dwarf and floating pond plants, which sit in the water. Bring tropical and subtropical plants indoors for winter. The pot should be protected from freezing as well. Floating pond plants survive cold weather in more temperate climates if the water garden is deep enough, but to be safe, overwinter them indoors. Alternatively, set up the potted water garden indoors and enjoy it year-round.

plants

1. plectranthus
2. jasmine
3. ornamental sweet potato vine
4. helichrysum 'lemon licorice'
5. lemongrass
6. fern

Though the sound of gently splashing water provides a source of contentment for many, the fountain and pump are optional features for a potted water garden. Plants are optional, too, for that matter. You may prefer to start with a large container of water that's quietly reflective. If so, keep algae under control by cleaning the container and replacing the water in it every couple of weeks. If you decide that you'd enjoy the entertainment, add a pump and fountain to your water garden. If you wish, add plants later.

plants and water

left and opposite:
Water pouring from the bamboo spout doesn't disturb the plants here because they grow in a container (a manger basket) set securely on the rim of the ceramic pot. Colorful lilies float at the edge of the pond as a decorative touch.

container gardens | **69**

potted water garden

1 **container and plants** Select a large container that holds about 35 gallons of water. A glazed ceramic pot works beautifully, but resin or fiberglass containers hold water, too. The subtropical plants shown here sit in a container at the water's edge; they must be wintered indoors. If you prefer pond plants that dwell in the water, choose from those listed *at right*. Once potted, set their containers directly in the water, placing them on bricks to achieve the appropriate depth.

2 **basket** Line the manger basket with a sheet of plastic, such as a lawn bag, and line that with the coconut-husk liner made to fit the frame. Add 3 inches of potting mix.

3 **plant** Remove plants from their nursery pots and arrange them in the planter. Place the largest plants in the center. Arrange the remaining plants evenly in the container, situating low-growing plants at the manger's edge. Sprinkle potting mix between the plants and covering the root balls. Top off the plantings with 2 inches of mix.

Make a tepee to support the climbing plants, starting with two of the bamboo stakes. Push a stake into the soil at each end of the basket, and then wire together the top ends of the stakes.

Cut the third bamboo stake in half and wire the half-length to the straight side of the basket and the tops of the other stakes, to add stability and to complete the tepee.

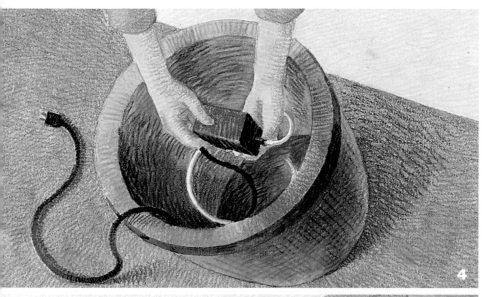

pump Before filling the pot with water, **4** move it to the desired location; you won't be able to move it when it's full of water. Choose a spot that receives morning sun.

Set a small water pump to the desired rate of flow. Set it in the bottom of the ceramic pot and drape the electrical cord over the side of the pot. The plants will conceal the cord. Connect the vinyl tubing at the base of the bamboo spout to the pump. Place the bamboo spout across the middle of the pot, with its ends resting on the rim.

finish Set the planter at one side of **5** the pot, behind the bamboo spout. Fill the pot with water to just past the bottom of the planter. Slide the bamboo spout next to the front of the planter. Plug the pump into a three-prong grounded (GFCI) outlet. If the water flows too swiftly or too gently from the spout, experiment with the rate of flow on the pump to arrive at a desired level.

Water plants when the soil feels dry and fertilize once a month. In hot weather, top off the water in the pot as needed.

In cold climates, dismantle the water garden in late fall, or bring the entire garden indoors for winter.

great plants for potted water gardens

- arrowhead
- caladium
- canna
- duckweed
- dwarf cattail
- dwarf papyrus
- harlequin flower
- parrot's feather

- miniature water lily
- siberian iris
- sweet flag
- water clover
- water fern
- water hyacinth
- water lettuce
- water snowflake

containers
for every
place

entries

welcome wagon
Make the first glimpse of your house a memorable one, whether you have plenty of space or a little. Fill pots and hanging baskets with brightly colored annuals and perennials. Set small shrubs and dwarf evergreen or deciduous trees in containers. Arrange the pots in groupings for seasonal displays. Include temporary plants for special holidays or occasions.

Rearranging plants in pots is much easier and more immediate than moving those in the ground. That ease provides you with the chance to experiment. Try plants different from those you might grow in a regular border and try new designs that combine the plants in unusual compositions in individual pots or groups of pots.

Plan ahead and consider how much sun your entry receives.

The walk leading to the house may be in full sun, for example. But if the entry itself has an overhanging porch roof or eaves, shade will predominate, even if the front yard faces south. Select plants accordingly for sun, light shade, or full shade. Remember to water plants often if they are placed by a sheltered door.

color up front
left and below: Put sun-lovers, such as these geraniums, in a decorative wagon, and then just pull it out of the shade of a porch or arbor and into the sun every few days.

plants

1 marigold
2 lobelia
3 geranium
4 petunia
5 pansy
6 grapevine

container gardens | **75**

entries

temporary touch

right: Use container plantings to fill in empty spaces in a newly landscaped front yard. The pots of color dress up the entryway until the in-ground plants spread and mature.

changeable accents

below left: Instead of covering an entry arbor with a climbing plant, show off the structure's design by hanging baskets of bright-hue annuals from the apex and securing pots to the top of an adjoining fence.

tropical splendor

below right: Take advantage of the temporary aspect of container gardening. Plant tropicals, such as abutilon, canna, and sweet potato vine, in a pot set near the house wall. The plants, which don't survive cold weather, will thrive through summer in the protected environment.

design accents

Welcome visitors at the entrance to your house with warm plantings that complement its style. Highlight design aspects of the house or entryway instead of camouflaging or ignoring them. Match the containers and their plants to the design, such as tropicals arrayed in front of a contemporary house. Use one large (24–inch wide) container overflowing with plants instead of several small pots. A large pot makes more of an impact, especially if it is unique or the plants in it are unusual.

inviting scene

left: Border an informal walk from the gate to the house with both planted and empty containers, such as the terra-cotta urns here. Allow the pots to protrude onto the walk, lending a sense of direction and discovery.

every space
Remember all the areas
around the front of
your house: Containers
go anywhere and
everywhere. Hang them
on or around the front
door and even above
the garage door.
Suspend baskets from
porch eaves. March
pots, like a double rank
of soldiers, along the
edges of the walk. Give
visitors an appetizing
glimpse of a garden
with potted edibles at
the entry gate or
around the garden itself
in place of a fence.

plant potential
right: **Picture this
scene without the
plants. Previously
rather barren looking,
it gains an English-
style country garden
feel from the
profusion of plants.
Enjoy the lush looks of
perennials and shrubs
that add to the effect
year after year with
minimal upkeep.**

edible journey

left: Lead guests into the garden and encourage them to nibble from the welcoming pots of red and green lettuces. Where garden space is lacking, set the pots conveniently outside the back door.

knock, knock

below left: Greet visitors with a pretty basket of flowers on your door. Select plants according to the amount of sun they'll receive; this front door with its basket of verbena gets morning sun— just enough to keep the flowers coming.

hang 'em high

below right: The blank space above a garage door makes a perfect planting opportunity. Suspend baskets of plants, such as petunias, lobelia, and vinca vine, above the door to break up the stark expanse that ordinarily faces you.

stairways

step up beautifully

Steps form the transition between a streetside walk and your front door, or lead the way from the back door out to a garden. Plants highlight this architectural element that's typically taken for granted.

Stairs offer excellent opportunities for container plantings because they're usually wider than walkways. Frame an entrance with containers lining the stairs. Some stairs offer landings for decorating; others have sturdy stoops, that easily accommodate planters or small window boxes.

plants

1 begonia

2 regal geranium

3 'star gazer' oriental hybrid lily

4 petunia

5 regal geranium

Break up a long run of stairs by placing planters here and there or off to the side.

Use pots to accentuate an architectural element, such as a railing post. Tempting as it may be, don't train a vining plant to twine around the only railing. If your stairway has two railings, grow a vine on one of them but leave a railing for people to hold onto. Safety considered, choose attractive vines, such as small-flowered clematis, black-eyed Susan vine, and Madeira vine. Morning glory and moon vine produce too many large leaves to suit a railing.

arrayed beauty
left and opposite:
A mass of gorgeous flowers parades up these wooden steps to an entry porch. Begonias, geraniums, petunias, and 'Star Gazer' lilies thrive in the morning sun here. Lilies grow surprisingly well in pots, and they make awesome accents to lower-growing plants. The profusion of color brightens the subdued hue of the house and provides a warm welcome to visitors. Transplant lilies to the garden when they finish blooming; they'll come back next year.

stairways

step wisely

Lining a flight of stepswith pots creates a welcome sight, but don't let them interfere with foot traffic. Strap pots to stair railing posts, if possible, to anchor them. Choose low, wide containers that won't tip over easily. Select low-growing plants that won't obstruct steps.

Clustered plantings, as well as plantings in large containers, retain moisture longer than individual or small pots. Upright pots full of dry soil blow over easily in a strong wind.

sun-dappled

above: Set an array of pots on one side of steps shaded by deciduous trees. Fill the containers with plants, such as cyclamen that appreciate the filtered sunlight. Double-pot the plants to replace them easily when they stop flowering.

shade-spotted

right: Brighten the steps or stoop of a northeast- or north-facing entry with low bowls of plants, such as impatiens, that thrive in shade.

in-town country

left: Who needs a yard? Create a cottage-garden look by planting a mass of annuals and perennials, including salvia, nasturtium, impatiens, and plectranthus, in a riot of colors. Use matching, or at least similar, containers to organize the design. Mix the plants in each container. These plants flower well in full or partial sun.

cuttings galore

below: Plant spring-flowering bulbs along the entrance to your garden and cut bouquets handily. In fall, tuck daffodil bulbs into large pots and the edges of beds. When the flowers finish blooming in spring, replace them with summer-flowering annuals, such as salvia, zinnia, and snapdragon.

container gardens | **83**

patios

easy living

Transforming your patio, courtyard, or terrace into a spectacular garden setting with dozens of colorful pots doesn't require much time or effort.

Take full advantage of the space when you design: Locate a potted kitchen garden of edible plants outside the back door. Place pockets of bright-color plants in corners or around the patio's perimeter. Define the space using permanent potted plantings, such as evergreen shrubs and ornamental grasses. Plant vertically, using walls and overhanging branches of trees as plant supports.

Hook up containers to a drip irrigation system, with one dripper for each pot, to eliminate the daily chore of watering in hot, dry weather. Select at least some of the plants for their drought tolerance.

color changes

left and below:
**Despite the challenges
and difficult growing
conditions of the
desert Southwest, this
garden blooms
nonstop there, entirely
in pots, from February
through May. As pots
packed with flowering
bulbs, annuals, and
perennials finish
blooming, they're
replaced.**

plants

1 geranium

2 marigold

3 hollyhock

4 petunia

5 jasmine

6 lobelia

container gardens | **85**

about color

The choice of color schemes for your container plantings depends on how you plan to use the patio. If you spend summer days there, bright colors add a lively, warm ambience. If you entertain often in the evening, white and silvery shades glow at dusk. Gardening in pots makes switching color schemes a snap. In late summer, replace spent annuals and herbs with cool-season stars, such as flowering kale, snapdragon, or pansy.

soothing hues

right: **This silver-and-white scheme blazes through autumn by combining chrysanthemums, flowering kale, variegated ivy, and dusty miller.**

edibles at hand

below left: **Pots of vegetables and herbs frame a patio with red, purple, and yellow highlights.**

hot combo

below right: **Alternanthera, deep pink petunia, and sweet potato vine harmonize beautifully and thrive in the shelter of a terrace wall.**

sunbathers

above: Cacti in terra-cotta planters bask atop a patio wall under the desert Southwest sun. The cacti bloom in spring, along with a Lady Banks rose that climbs the adobe wall.

color coordinates

left: It doesn't matter which came first here: the gaily painted chair, the vivid pots, or the plants (which include marigolds, sunflowers, and hot peppers). The effect is as hot as spicy salsa. Adapt this design to your furniture, blending cool hues of blue, lavender, and white or hot shades of red, yellow, and orange.

potting spot

A corner of the patio or terrace makes an ideal location for a potting bench. Imagine transplanting plants and potting seedlings within steps of the garden. You'll enjoy the fresh air and won't concern yourself with spilling soil on the floor or ruining a rug.

Let your potting bench do double duty as a buffet when serving a family meal or entertaining; or use it as a place to display decorative objects or potted plants out of reach of little hands.

stocking up

Of course, you're going to use a potting bench most often for planting. Though your specific needs may vary, a few essential items prove handy for most gardeners: Stock various sizes of practical and decorative pots, from 2½ inches wide for transplanting seedlings to 12-inch or larger planters. Keep various saucers and pot feet on hand

to use with those pots. Store hand tools, such as trowels, cultivators, bulb planters, pruners, scissors, twine, plant ties, plant labels, and a permanent marker. Place bags or boxes of fertilizer in the bins, as well as the components of your soil mixes, such as potting soil, vermiculite, perlite, sphagnum, peat moss, and compost. Store a package of water-retentive polymer crystals here, too.

A deep open bin at one end of the potting bench provides a place to keep long-handled tools easily accessible.

outdoor organizer

opposite: A potting bench with covered bins presents a neat appearance while hiding soil mixes, fertilizers, and simple clutter. Add a shelf to display a few plants or an artful arrangement of empty clay pots. Pegs in the top of the potting bench frame make handy hooks for hanging hand tools.

handy storage

left: With the lid of the bench raised, the compartments, which normally hold soil or tools, become handy caddies for ice and soft drinks when you entertain. With the lid closed, serving pieces or attractive plant arrangements find a convenient spot for display when not in use.

decks & balconies

outdoor rooms

Turn an ordinary deck or balcony into an exquisite outdoor dining room for entertaining or relaxing. Adding structure, via a pergola and railings, creates a ceiling for protection from the elements and walls for privacy. However, these elements also offer places for plants, whether you add built-in planters and climbing plants or large pots of colorful bloomers. A simple wood-frame awning or lattice provides a comparable place for plants to climb and enlivens the room. When you step out onto the deck or balcony, you'll feel as if you're stepping into the garden.

When planting in containers on a deck or a patio, remember that the larger the container, the less often you'll need to water. The structure must

in the midst of nature

right and below: **Partly shaded by surrounding trees, this deck brings nature up close with plants in containers and even a living chandelier (hanging basket). A wisteria vine will mature and soften the hard edges of the pergola over time.**

plants

1 variegated ivy

2 wisteria

3 geranium

4 ivy

5 impatiens

6 begonia

be able to support the weight of the planters: soil, plants, and all. Plant seasonal combinations of annuals and change them as the blooms fade. Or, go for more permanent plantings of perennials, especially fragrant perennials or tropical bloomers that can be wintered indoors if your climate dictates. Set planters on wheels to make them more mobile.

integral color
above: **When building a deck, incorporate places for plants in the design from the beginning. This shallow, rectangular planter is set into the deck floor. Finished to match the railings and built-in seats, it fills a corner of the deck with your favorite colorful annuals and fragrant herbs.**

decks & balconies

multiple uses

Potted plants accessorize a deck as attractively as more traditional items, such as statuary. Given the limited free space you find on a deck, and even less on a balcony, choice pots and combinations of plants provide just the right finishing touch. Consider the limitations as opportunities for creating terrific pocket gardens of edibles or miniature roses, for example. Experiment with arranging themed gardens: a few pots with plants that attract birds in one corner, a large planter filled with tropical beauties in another.

formal touch

right: **A potted dwarf Alberta spruce and herb topiaries dress up an outdoor area for entertaining on a deck. The plants move indoors over winter. Combine the potted plants with cushy seating and a panoramic view for the perfect setting.**

for the birds

left: A birdbath-turned-water garden forms a focal point among the colorful plants set against a deck railing.

tropical look

below left: For height, plant a container with zebra grass and annuals, such as flowering tobacco and coleus, without obstructing the view.

rosy outlook

below right: Hung on a shared balcony railing, miniature roses bring country to the city.

rooftops

bird's-eye view

Up on a rooftop, containers provide the only way to surround yourself with flowers and foliage. Select large planters (at least 24 inches in diameter) for full-size trees, lightweight window boxes for the perimeter, hanging baskets for overhead trellises or pergolas, and smaller pots for herbs and annuals. Use lightweight potting mixes and check building codes before you plant.

Plants enable you to create an unexpected oasis in the midst of a city. Frame a good view, or hide an unattractive one, with potted trees and plant-shrouded arbors. Use plants to create wind buffers. Water diligently.

rooftop oasis

right and opposite: **Accent your sky-high haven with perennials and annuals. Secure planters to the top of the walls surrounding the area.**

fire escape fancy

above: Baskets of geraniums hang beneath the fire escape, making it possible to water them from the steps above. While the plants soften the immovable hardscape, they also create privacy without obstructing foot traffic.

plants

1 verbena

2 impatiens

3 miniature rose

4 russian sage

5 pentas

6 mandevilla

7 cleome

8 black-eyed susan

9 petunia

container gardens | **95**

containers in the garden

defining art

Large or small, any garden benefits from potted plantings. Placed strategically, large containers create strong focal points. As architectural elements, they add structure and form instantly. Combining a simple, four-legged obelisk and twining clematis with a square planter, for instance, makes a handsome, living sculpture.

Use rows of pots to define the perimeter of a garden bed, to form a wall to screen an unattractive view, or to mark steps in the garden. Brighten a shady spot under trees with containers of light-color plants. Place containers in the garden as permanent features or temporary ones. When lightweight enough to be movable, a large pot of colorful blooms creates drama and intrigue.

functional forms

above and right: Planters with obelisks add structure and height to the garden while helping to define planting areas as well as pathways. The large, empty amphora in the center of the bisecting paths anchors the design. The potted evergreen stands at left in the garden.

zones	time	skill
3–11	weekend	moderate

you will need

2×2s: four
5–6-ft. lengths of
cedar or redwood;
one 2-in.×2-in.
cube for core

decorative finial

2-in. deck screws

circular saw

wood stain or
exterior latex paint
(optional)

drill with ¼-in. bit

galvanized fence
staples or screw
eyes (optional)

nylon wire or
string (optional)

build an obelisk

Add vertical interest to a garden with supports such as tepees, obelisks, and trellises. These structures provide extra growing space for even the smallest garden. Adapt the height of the uprights (or legs) to suit the size of the containers. Use three- or four-legged tepees to support your choice of climbing plants. Obelisks look as good unadorned as they do with plants twining their way up and around the legs. Trellises made with lumber, lattice, or netting supply toeholds for plants that climb naturally as well as those that need a helping hand to begin their growth.

lend a hand

right: **Assist vines, such as this Jackman clematis in climbing an obelisk by criss-crossing nylon twine up the legs. Use screw eyes to hold the twine in place.**

great plants for climbing and vining

- black-eyed susan vine
- canary vine
- carolina jessamine
- clematis
- climbing rose
- honeysuckle
- ivy
- jasmine
- madeira vine
- mandevilla
- moonflower
- morning glory
- nasturtium
- passionflower
- sweet pea
- trumpet vine

showing off

above: One advantage of pairing clematis with an obelisk is that its twining stems usually do not completely cover the support. The structure, whether obelisk or trellis, remains an important part of the planting's overall design.

details, details

Vary the height of this easy-to-build obelisk from 5 to 6 feet tall. Make the height of the finished structure in scale with the size of your planter. Predrill starter holes in the top and sides of a 2×2 cube. Cut each top and bottom of the 2×2 legs at a 15-degree angle; join the top ends by attaching them to the sides of the cube using deck screws. Screw the finial into the top of the cube. Paint or seal the lumber before assembling, or leave it unfinished to weather naturally. Insert the obelisk legs at least 4 to 6 inches deep in the soil-filled planter.

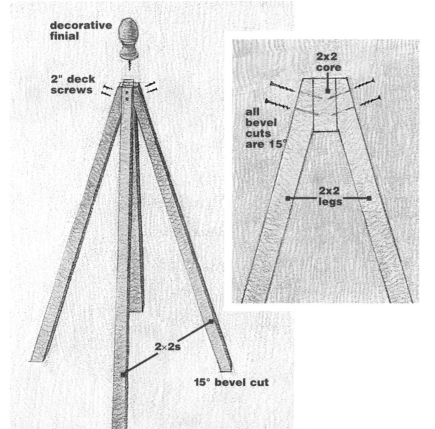

decorative finial

2" deck screws

all bevel cuts are 15°

2x2 core

2x2 legs

2×2s

15° bevel cut

container gardens | **99**

surprise accents

Plants in containers, especially bold or unusual containers, make delightful surprise additions to in-ground plantings. Highlight a favorite plant such as godetia *(below right)* by placing it in a pot on a pedestal amid surrounding perennials. Containers fit almost anywhere, so you don't need much vacant space in a border to plop one or two down. Set a pot of yellow coreopsis in a tangle of red pincushion *(Knautia)*, black-eyed Susan, and tawny daylily. Prop a planter of blue salvia and white nicotiana on top of an overturned pot in place of a recently deceased plant. Place a planted urn or shallow bowl at the turn of a curving path. Slightly hide the planters in a border or, for a more pronounced effect, cluster them at the edge of plantings.

contrasts

above right: Ruffled echeveria, with its round rosettes of bluish leaves, contrasts with the green, sword-shape foliage of nearby perennials.

highlights

right: Use a pedestal to showcase a planter and its contents, such as the pink godetia and blue lobelia here, amidst taller, in-ground plants.

decorative edging

left: Cinderblocks, with their pot-size openings, hold drought-tolerant plants, such as succulents, herbs, and zinnias. Their compact size makes them perfect for edging perennial beds, a vegetable plot, or the perimeter of a patio.

spot color

below: Red dahlias in a bright blue pot add exuberant color at the corner of a perennial border. Strategically locate tender plants, such as these, for easy removal at the first sign of frost in fall.

shady pots

right: In the light shade of a shallow-root tree where grass won't grow, group pots of caladium, begonia, impatiens, and sweet alyssum. Just as you mix and match plants in a garden, combine pot shapes and sizes when grouping containers in the garden, too.

standing ovation

below: What's so exciting about an empty pot? Everything, when the container is as imposing and graceful as this one. Such a large vessel, whether a simple pot or a more stylized urn, doesn't need embellishment. Artful containers become stars in the garden when they're allowed to shine. Surround them with a supportive cast of a few plants with simple aesthetics to complete the staging, then set up seating nearby where you'll enjoy the serene view.

true reflection

left: Sky-blue pots arranged along the edge of a pond add color and formality to the design. In combination with larger terra-cotta planters, they add structural interest to the pond but create a barrier that helps keep curious kids and pets from getting too close to the water's edge.

focal point

left: Water—still or splashing—is such an important part of a garden. It often becomes the finishing touch that transforms an acceptable but ordinary design into a very special creation. Even though potted water gardens exist on their own very well, they also merge beautifully with surrounding plants. Turn a container into a water garden and make it the focal point of a meandering garden bed. The blooming water lilies here are an asset but are not necessary to draw a visitor's attention away from the ornamental grasses, cycad, and geranium and toward the burnished container.

the basics

soil

soil savvy

Success begins with soil. This mantra for gardeners also applies when gardening in containers. Faced with a choice between garden soil and a high-quality packaged potting soil, opt for the latter. Garden soil typically contains weed seeds and is heavy, especially when wet.

Your choice of a commercial potting mix for planters may not contain soil. Called soilless mix, it may contain peat moss, vermiculite, and other ingredients that make it lighter in weight than garden soil. This is important especially when you plan to hang baskets and window boxes. Use a lightweight potting mix for more portable pots.

Most packaged potting soils work well in planters. They also make an excellent base for any blend that you'd like to customize for your plants. Choose ingredients based on plants' needs for moisture and drainage.

customize the mix

above: Blend your own potting medium as an alternative to purchasing packaged potting soil. Vary the ingredients according to plants' needs. Customize a mix for containers by adding perlite (to increase drainage) and water-absorbing polymer crystals (to help the blend retain moisture). If you prefer, add peat moss or leaf mold (to boost the water-holding capacity of the mix) and vermiculite (to lighten it).

make it ideal

right: The best soil is rich in organic matter, such as compost and rotted manure. Add these sources of nitrogen and other nutrients to your potting mix. Adding organic matter improves soil drainage, too. This is significant; if plant roots sit in heavy, saturated soil, they rot. Your choice of potting mix should offer adequate drainage.

container potting mixes

soil type	contents/plants
all-purpose	sterilized soil, sand or perlite, peat moss/annuals, vegetables, trees, and shrubs
soilless	sphagnum peat moss, perlite or sand, vermiculite, compost or dried manure/temporary plants, such as annuals and vegetables
water-retentive	all-purpose mix plus water-retentive crystals/almost any plant except cacti and succulents
well-drained	sterilized soil, peat moss, sand, leaf mold, grit/woodland and alpine plants
acidic	all-purpose mix with added peat moss or ground pine or fir bark/ericaceous plants, such as azalea, rhododendron, pieris, and heather
cacti	sterilized soil, sand, vermiculite, gravel, ground limestone/cacti and succulents

Water and drainage play a key role in the effectiveness of a potting mix and therefore in the health and vigor of your plantings. Hard water raises the pH of soil, making it more alkaline. This characteristic does not bother many plants but is definitely detrimental to acid-loving ones, such as rhododendrons, azaleas, and heathers. Adding perlite to any mix lightens it and improves drainage because the styrene particles do not absorb water. They instead create spaces through which water flows.

When blending your own potting mediums, moisten the vermiculite and peat moss with warm water before adding them to the mix. Once saturated, they're easier to manage and blend with other ingredients. Make enough potting mix to keep plenty on hand.

planting

a few guidelines

To save time and effort, use large containers at least 12 inches in diameter and 10 inches deep. The bigger the pot, the less often you'll need to water. The deeper the pot, the more room for root growth and the better your plants will perform.

Before planting, consider the mature size of the plants in relation to the overall size of the container. Large plants need correspondingly large planters. By the same token, just as a diminutive plant may get lost in the garden, a small plant calls for a container of an appropriately smaller volume.

Design your potted garden with the same considerations you have for an in-ground garden: Graduate heights, mix foliage textures and bloom colors, and group plants with similar cultural requirements. Choose long-blooming annuals or combine perennials with various bloomtimes, staggering them for the longest show. When potting perennials with short-lived blooms, tuck in longer-blooming annuals around them to extend the display of flowers.

Before planting terra-cotta or other porous pots, soak them in water. Dry pots absorb moisture from the soil, robbing from the plants.

Prepare to plant by filling containers half- to three-quarters full with soil. Sprinkle a slow-release fertilizer on top of the soil and mix it in thoroughly. Begin planting by placing the tallest plants off to one side for an asymmetrical look, at the center for a symmetrical design. Next, plant bushy, medium-height perennials and annuals. Finish with trailing plants along the edge. Fill in between the plants with soil as you work. Leave an inch or two between the soil surface and the rim of the container to allow for watering.

layer by layer

above: To combine plants in a large container, put a few inches of potting mix in the bottom. First, place the tallest, largest plant in the center. Add enough mix to set bushy, medium-height, and trailing plants nearer to the top of the planter, keeping them at a depth comparable to their nursery pots.

recycle

above: Make use of empty aluminum soft drink cans that won't rust. Place them in the bottom of very large containers to help lighten the load and make the pot easier to move around.

root-bound plants

above left: When purchasing plants, check to see if they're root-bound. Roots encircle the soil, indicating that the plants have been growing in the same small pot for too long. Before transplanting into a slightly larger container, gently work around the sides and bottom of the root ball to loosen the roots, encouraging outward growth rather than the strangling pattern. The same tendency in a more mature plant tells you it's time to repot it in a larger container, too.

starting from seed

above right: Many plants grow easily from seed when sown directly in the container: basil, cilantro, bachelor's buttons, cosmos, marigolds, carrots, beets, and lettuces. Smooth the top of the planting medium, sprinkle seeds on the surface, and cover with more medium to the depth recommended on the packet. Keep the medium evenly moist until the seeds germinate.

propping up

left: Provide a cage or hoop support for taller plants, such as lilies, which tend to flop over in heavy rain or wind, to keep them upright. Vining plants also need a structure to climb on. Insert or attach these supports at planting time. As the plant grows, it camouflages the framework.

container gardens | **109**

watering

crucial for success

In any garden, consistent watering translates into healthy plants. But water is crucial to the survival of potted gardens. In the ground, plants spread their roots out and down in search of moisture, but in containers they can't go very far.

Diligently check soil moisture by poking a finger into soil to feel if it is dry. Water once or twice a day during hot, dry weather, every other day during cooler periods, and less often when rain waters plants for you. Make watering part of your usual stroll around the garden. Groom plants as you go, removing spent blooms and leaves as well as checking for pests and disease.

Your containers must have drainage holes so plants won't be sitting in water, especially after rainy spells. Place saucers under pots to catch and hold rain or excess water until it evaporates or the

design a system

above: **Drip irrigation kits work for hanging baskets as well as standing pots. Group pots of the thirstiest plants.**

perky pots

right: **Set pot feet—or decorative blocks of wood—under pots. This raises pots up enough to provide air circulation and discourage sow bugs, and it prevents the surface of patios and decks from staining.**

pot and soil gradually absorb it.

Plants that wilt repeatedly indicate stress. They won't grow well or flower as beautifully as you would like, and they'll be more susceptible to pests and diseases.

Though some plants grow well with minimal water, you may find that installing drip irrigation designed for containers works best for all your plants. Even when you're pressed for time or on vacation, they'll be watered consistently by a system set up with a timer to turn

protect the surface

above left: Mulch the soil surface of potted plants to help maintain soil moisture. Use decorative mulches, such as pea gravel, coarse sand, or river rocks. Moss and coconut husk work well, too. Remember that clay pots lose moisture more quickly than containers made of less porous materials, such as fiberglass and resin.

reinforce the soil

above right: Mix water-retentive, polymer crystals into soil at planting time. The crystals absorb water and expand, and then release moisture gradually as the soil dries.

lessen the chore

left: Drip irrigation helps water plants regularly and efficiently. Place one emitter in the middle of each container.

fertilizing

meals to go

Time-release organic fertilizers provide an ideal food for plants in containers. Organic fertilizers depend on soil microbes to activate them and release their nutrients gradually to plants. Compost and rotted manure provide nitrogen and other nutrients that plants need for healthy growth. These organic amendments improve soil drainability as well. Other sources of nitrogen include blood meal, cottonseed meal, fish meal, and fish emulsion. Rock phosphate and potash provide the other key nutrients that plants require, phosphorous and potassium. Buy bags of premixed, balanced organic fertilizer and use it in addition to organic amendments to build healthy soil. Follow the label directions for amounts to use in containers. Feed when you plant and monthly thereafter.

midseason break

right: **Give plants a nutritional boost in midseason by sprinkling fertilizer on top of the soil and lightly scratching it in with a cultivator.**

a cuppa nutrition

right: **Make green manure tea by steeping a large bunch of comfrey leaves in a 5-gallon bucket of water for several days. Strain and pour the richly nutritious tea around the base of plants.**

handle with care

far right: **Yellowing foliage may indicate that soil lacks vital nutrients. Use a soil tester to correct any deficiencies.**

stocking up

Many of the tools you use for tending your garden also simplify container gardening tasks. You don't need long-handled tools, although a spade proves useful for blending large batches of potting mix in a wheelbarrow. Hand tools with extended-reach handles ease most tasks. As with any type of gardening, a trowel makes the most indispensible tool for planting. Attach a watering wand to the end of your hose to make watering easier.

The advantage to gardening in containers, however, is that you usually work on a small scale. Improvise, if you want, and borrow tools from the kitchen. Tablespoons and forks work well when cultivating the soil in pots or scratching in fertilizer, for instance.

A dibble, or bulb-planting tool, comes in handy when working with container plantings. Use one to make planting holes or to loosen soil.

essential tools

bulb planter	trowel
5-gallon bucket	watering can
hand cultivator	watering wand
heavy-duty scissors	weeder
pruner	wheelbarrow

good as new

left: Give your hand tools, such as trowels and cultivators, a longer life by keeping them clean and rust-free. After use, wipe soil from tools, then dunk them in a bucket of sand mixed with ½ cup of ordinary motor oil. Remove rust spots with steel wool.

winterizing

getting set for the cold

With the exception of a few areas of the country, the imminent onset of winter means scurrying to protect plants in the gardens from the ravages of freezing and thawing. Before that last-minute rush, however, plan to move all your tender container plants indoors. Those include herbs, such as rosemary and bay, as well as tender perennials (blue salvia, for instance) and annuals (geraniums, marigolds, and begonias) that you'd like to keep flowering through the winter. Annuals survive best if you root stem cuttings instead of bringing in whole plants. Move plants indoors before night temperatures lower to the 50s and before you turn

tender pots

right: Protect empty pots from snow and freezing rain by moving them into a garage, a shed, or a basement at the end of the growing season. Clean pots before placing them in storage; you'll avoid that chore during the busier spring season.

clean up

right: Use steel wool and vinegar to wash off fertilizer salts.

tender plants

far right: Tender trees, perennials, and shrubs, including rosemary *(shown)* and bay survive winter outdoors only in warm climates. These delicate plants die when exposed to freezing temperatures, so move them indoors in late summer or early fall and enjoy them as houseplants until spring, when they return to the garden.

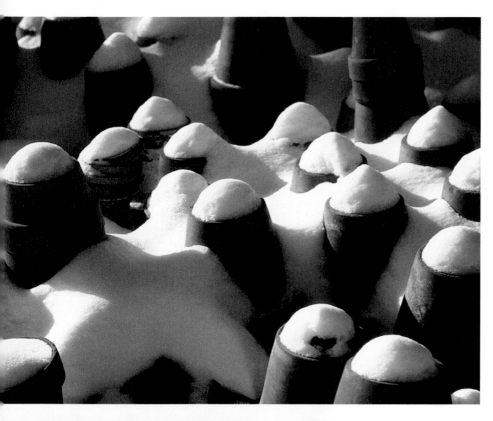

weatherworn

above: Snow capped pots look pretty, but inexpensive planters deteriorate quickly in severe weather conditions.

chipped away

left: Repetitive freezing and thawing damages ordinary clay pots. The result is chipped and flaking edges and bottoms.

the heat on. Plants that have spent the summer outdoors need time to adjust to the indoor environment; dry, hot air from heating systems makes that acclimation more difficult.

Potted perennials, shrubs, and trees left outdoors year-round require protection not only from frigid temperatures but also from the alternating periods of freezing and thawing that can cause plants to heave (push up and out of the soil) and possibly injure them. Potted plants heave out of their soil, too. Some kinds of containers, including terra-cotta, concrete, and ceramic, generally don't tolerate winter ravages well, either.

Safeguard container plantings by enclosing them with a cylinder of chicken wire filled with dried leaves or straw. Alternatively, wrap pots with lengths of burlap until they're well-insulated. Nestle these pots against a sunny side of the house to keep them sheltered and warmer than they would be in an exposed location.

If you prefer, move planters, particularly those on decks and patios, into an unheated shed or garage. Set pots in large boxes packed with styrene packing pieces to help insulate them. Use a dolly, wheelbarrow, or carrying poles to transport large, heavy pots and protect your back from strain.

Protect broad- and needle-leaf evergreens from moisture loss by spraying them with an antitranspirant. Use the product before daytime temperatures sink regularly below 45 degrees.

In climates where long-term freezing is inevitable, equip yourself with plenty of old bedsheets or lightweight blankets to cover plants at night and protect them through cold spells until freezing weather sets in. In milder climates (Zones 7 and warmer) these covers prove useful from time to time to get your plants through a cold snap.

In all areas, have patience in spring. Wait until the nighttime air temperatures stay consistently above 50 degrees before removing winter wraps.

tips

1 **lighten up** Large pots become heavy and practically immovable when filled with soil and water. Make them more portable by placing an inverted plastic nursery pot on the bottom of the planter and filling in around it with soil. You won't need to expend as much effort lugging the container around, and you'll save money by needing less soil to fill the container. The nursery pot won't interfere with plant roots.

Water will drain from the soil through the holes in the bottom of the nursery pot. If the possibility of waterlogged soil bothers you, raise the nursery pot up a fraction by setting it on top of a few pot shards, but don't block the drainage holes in the larger container when you do so.

2 **drill drainage holes** The most common cause of plant death in containers is waterlogged soil. Containers without drainage holes foster soggy soil. Though most pots come with drainage holes, many decorative containers do not. Remedy that situation, if you wish, by drilling one or more holes in the bottom of your container. It's easy enough to drill through clay, ceramic, resin, fiberglass, and wood planters. Use a drill with an appropriate bit made for masonry or wood, and wear protective goggles to protect your eyes from small flying specks. Place a cross of masking tape over the spot where you plan to drill to prevent the pot from cracking as you drill.

To puncture drainage holes in the bottom of metal containers, use a large nail and hammer. One or two small holes are better than none.

finger saver When you plant or **3** repot a spiny cactus, wear impermeable gloves. For further protection from the prickly spines, roll up a sheet of newspaper and use it like a pair of tongs. Wrap it around the plant to lift, hold, and settle the plant in its new home.

furry delight Give your feline friends **4** their own potted garden. Entice them by planting catnip in a large planter such as a wooden half-barrel, where there's room for kitty to lie and roll among the leaves. By containing catnip, a gregarious member of the mint family, you'll keep it from running rampant in the garden.

summer vacation Remember your **5** potted plants when you plan your vacation. To help them survive while you're away, move them into a place protected from the direct sun and wind (under the eaves of the house or the garage, for example, or in the light shade of a large tree). Water the plants thoroughly before you leave.

If you will be gone for more than a week, set the pots on top of bricks or stones inside large saucers or tubs. Pour 2 inches of water into this reservoir until the water reaches the bottom of the pot.

If you have only a few containers, ask a neighbor to check them and water as necessary.

Before you go away, harvest mature and nearly ripe fruit and vegetables to keep plants in the production mode.

container gardens | **117**

6 **multiplication** Many plants root readily from stem cuttings. It's an easy way to increase a collection of favorites. In addition to scented geraniums (*shown*), try any of these:

artemisia	lemon balm
chrysanthemum	rosemary
helichrysum	sage
impatiens	swedish ivy
ivy	sweet potato vine
ivy geranium	zonal geranium

Make stem cuttings by snipping 4- to 5-inch pieces from the ends of plant stems. Remove bottom sets of leaves. Dip the stem ends into a powdered rooting hormone. Stick the cuttings into moistened germinating mix in a flat. Place the flat outdoors in the shade or indoors on a sunny windowsill. Keep the mix evenly moist while the cuttings root. Resistance when you tug gently on the plants, or evidence of new growth from the top, indicates that the cuttings have rooted.

7 **say no to shards** Recent studies conducted by Cooperative Extension services across the country show that placing pot shards at the bottom of a container hinders rather than helps drainage. Unless the drainage hole is very large (more than 1 inch across) soil probably won't leak through the hole. Place a 2-inch square of old window screen over the hole to prevent soil loss.

Placing shards in the bottom of a container creates a space for the water to collect. Roots grow out of the soil into the waterlogged area, exposing them to oversaturation and risking rot.

get a good start Help your plants **8** overcome the shock of transplant and give them a boost toward good health. Just before you plant, gently dip the root ball (soil and all) in a bucket of water that contains a solution of B vitamins made for plants, available at nurseries and garden centers. Follow product label directions.

pest patrol Inspect your potted **9** plants regularly, watching for signs of pests or disease, such as weak growth, chewed or discolored leaves, and undeveloped flower buds. Once you have accurately identified the pest or disease that is plaguing a plant, look for a simple solution rather than a toxic chemical approach.

Remove diseased plants from containers and dispose of them in the trash (not the compost); replace them. Avoid spreading disease among plants by washing your hands after handling them. Scrub containers.

Deal easily with insect pests, such as aphids (*shown*), by blasting them off plants using cold water from a hose. Use an organic solution, such as Safer insecticidal soap, to deal with a range of pests, from spider mites to whiteflies and aphids, without threatening beneficial insects.

save your back Take advantage of **10** lightweight pots that resemble stone, terracotta, and concrete. Made of resin, fiberglass, or polystyrene, they're easy to move around, withstand all kinds of weather, and last for years. They come in a wide variety of colors and styles.

great plants for containers

annuals

Annuals flower for months–from spring to the first fall frosts–and provide continuous color in containers. Because they do not live from one year to the next, use them as the basis for temporary forays into unusual combinations and designs. Experiment. They're glorious individually and grouped.

***Heliotropium arbortescens* cultivars**
heliotrope

Hypoestes phyllostachya
pink polka-dot plant

- *Ageratum* species and cultivars
  ageratum
  ✽H:9 in.; S:6 in.; Z:all ●●●○

- *Alternanthera ficoideus* and cultivars
  copperleaf
  ✽◐H:18 in.; S:10 in.; Z:all ○●●

- *Antirrhinum majus*
  snapdragon
  ✽H:12 in.; S: 8 in.; Z:all ●●●●●○

- *Begonia semperflorens* cultivars
  wax begonia
  ✽◐H:8 in.; S:6 in.; Z:all ○●●○●

- *Brachycome iberidifolia*
  swan river daisy
  ✽H:12 in.; S:9 in.; Z:all ●●○

- *Brassica oleracea*
  ornamental kale
  ✽◐H:10 in.; S:12 in.; Z:all ●●●○○

- *Calendula officinalis*
  pot marigold
  ✽H:24 in.; S:12 in.; Z:3-8 ○●

- *Catharanthus roseus* cultivars
  madagascar periwinkle
  ✽◐H:20 in.; S:12 in.; Z:all ●●○

- *Centaurea cyanus* and cultivars
  dwarf bachelor's button
  ✽H:12 in.; S:8 in.; Z:all ●●●●○

- *Clarkia amoena*
  godetia
  ✽H:24 in.; S:24 in.; Z:all ●●○

- *Cosmos* species
  dwarf cosmos
  ✽H:30 in.; S:20 in.; Z:all ○●●●●○

- *Dianthus barbatus* cultivars
  sweet william
  ✽◐H:18 in.; S:12 in.; Z:all ●●●○

- *Gerbera jamesonii*
  gerbera daisy
  ✽H:18 in.; S:18 in.; Z:all ○●●○

- *Gomphrena globosa*
  globe amaranth
  ✽H:20 in.; S:12 in.; Z:all ●●●●○

- *Helianthus annuus*
  dwarf sunflower
  ✽H:36 in.; S:15 in.; Z:all ○●●○

- *Heliotropium arborescens* cultivars
  heliotrope
  ✽◐H:24 in.; S:18 in.; Z:all ●●○

- *Hypoestes phyllostachya*
  pink polka-dot plant
  ◐H:18 in.; S:12 in.; Z:all ●●●●

- *Impatiens walleriana* cultivars
  impatiens
  ✽◐H:15 in.; S:15 in.; Z:all ○●●●●○

***Pelargonium* species and cultivars**
scented geranium

***petunia* cultivars**
petunia

***Plectranthus* cultivars**
swedish ivy

key: ✽=sun; ✽=shade; ◐=part sun, part shade; H=height; S=spread; Z=zone;
bloom/foliage/fruit colors: ○=yellow; ●=red; ●=orange; ●=purple; ●=lavender; ●=blue; ●=pink; ○=white;
●=variegated; ●=silver/gray

Salvia species
salvia

Scaevola aemula
fan flower

Senecio cineraria
dusty miller

- *Lantana* species and cultivars
  lantana
  ✺◑H:18 in.; S:18 in.; Z:all ◐●●●●

- *Lobularia maritima* cultivars
  sweet alyssum
  ✺H:10 in.; S:12 in.; Z:all ●●●○

- *Nemesia strumosa* cultivars
  nemesia
  ✺H:12 in.; S:6 in.; Z:all ●●●●●○

- *Nicotiana alata*
  flowering tobacco
  ✺◑●H:24 in.; S:10 in.; Z:all ●●●●○

- *Pelargonium* x *hortorum*
  geranium
  ✺H:18 in.; S:12 in.; Z:all ●●●●○

- *Pelargonium* species and cultivars
  scented geranium
  ✺H:24 in.; S:30 in.; Z:all ●●○◑

- *Pentas lanceolata* cultivars
  egyptian star cluster (pentas)
  ✺H:18 in.; S:12 in.; Z:all ●●●●

- *Petunia* cultivars
  petunia
  ✺H:24 in.; S:18 in.; Z:all ●●●●●○

- *Plectranthus* cultivars
  swedish ivy
  ✺◑H:30 in.; S:24 in.; Z:all ●●●

- *Portulaca grandiflora*
  moss rose
  ✺H:8 in.; S:18 in.; Z:all ●●●●○

- *Salvia* species
  salvia
  ✺◑H:18 in.; S:12 in.; Z:all ●●●●

- *Scaevola aemula*
  fan flower
  ✺◑H:10 in.; S:18 in.; Z:all ●●●●

- *Senecio cineraria*
  dusty miller
  ✺H:12 in.; S:24 in.; Z: all ●

- *Solenostemon scutellarioides*
  coleus
  ✺◑H:18 in.; S:12 in.; Z: all ●●●●●

- *Tagetes* species and cultivars
  marigold
  ✺H:12 in.; S:8 in.; Z: all ○●●

- *Thymophylla tenuiloba*
  dahlberg daisy
  ✺H:12 in.; S:8 in.; Z: all ●

- *Viola* x *wittrockiana* species and cultivars
  pansy
  ✺◑H:8 in.; S:12 in.; Z: all ●●●●●●○

- *Zinnia* species and cultivars
  dwarf zinnia
  ✺H:12 in.; S:20 in.; Z: all ●●●●●○

Solenostemon scutellarioides
coleus

Tagetes species and cultivars
marigold

Viola wittrockiana species and cultivars
pansy

perennials

Most perennials survive for years in the garden or in containers. However, they bloom for a shorter time than annuals, so consider color and texture of foliage and plant habits as much as you do flower shades when selecting perennials for your planters. Their ephemeral blooms are worth the planning.

Agapanthus africanas and cultivars
lily-of-the-nile

Bambusa
bamboo

- *Achillea* species and cultivars
  yarrow
  ❀H:24 in.; S:18 in.; Z:3-10 ●●●○

- *Adiantum pedatum*
  maidenhair fern
  ❀H:18 in.; S:18 in.; Z:3-9 ●

- *Agapanthus orientalis* and cultivars
  lily-of-the-nile
  ❀◗H:36 in.; S:24 in.; Z:7-10 ●●○

- *Aquilegia* species and cultivars
  columbine
  ❀◗H:18 in.; S:12 in.; Z:3-9 ●●●●●●○

- *Armeria maritima*
  sea pink (thrift)
  ❀H:8 in.; S:12 in.; Z:4-9 ●●○

- *Artemisia* species and cultivars
  artemisia
  ❀H:24 in.; S:24 in.; Z:3-8 ●

- *Aster* species and cultivars
  aster
  ❀H:24 in.; S:18 in.; Z:3-8 ●●●●●○

- *Astilbe chinensis* 'Pumila'
  astilbe
  ◗H:12 in.; S:12 in.; Z:4-8 ●

- *Athyrium filix-femina*
  lady fern
  ❀H:30 in.; S:30 in.; Z:3-9 ●

- *Bambusa, Chusquea, Sasaellia*
  bamboo (clumping types)
  ❀◗H:8 ft.; S:4 ft.; Z:6-9 ●

- *Begonia grandis evansiana*
  hardy begonia
  ❀H:18 in.; S:18 in.; Z:7-9 ●●●●○●

- *Campanula* species and cultivars
  bellflower
  ❀◗H:12 in.; S:18 in.; Z:3-8 ●●●○

- *Carex morrowii*
  sedge
  ❀H:12 in.; S:18 in.; Z:7-10 ●

- *Cerastium tomentosum*
  snow-in-summer
  ❀H:8 in.; S:12 in.; Z:3-9 ○●

- *Chrysanthemum* cultivars
  chrysanthemum
  ❀H:24 in.; S:18 in.; Z:6-9 ●●●●●○

- *Coreopsis* species and cultivars
  coreopsis
  ❀◗H:24 in.; S:12 in.; Z:3-8 ●●○

- *Cyclamen hederifolium*
  hardy cyclamen
  ❀H:4 in.; S:10 in.; Z:5-9 ●○●

- *Dianthus* species and cultivars
  pinks
  ❀◗H:12 in.; S:12 in.; Z:4-9 ●●●●●○

Coreopsis species and cultivars
coreopsis

Dianthus species and cultivars
pinks

Digitalis
foxglove

key: ❀=sun; ❀=shade; ◗=part sun, part shade; H=height; S=spread; Z=zone

bloom/foliage/fruit colors: ●=yellow; ●=red; ●=orange; ●=purple; ●=lavender; ●=blue; ●=pink; ○=white; ●=variegated; ●=silver/gray

Felicia amelloides
blue daisy

Fuchsia cultivars
fuchsia 'gartenmeister'

- *Digitalis*
  foxglove
  ✺H:24 in.; S:12 in.; Z:4-9 ●●●○

- *Felicia amelloides*
  blue daisy
  ✺H:18 in.; S:36 in.; Z:9-11 ●

- *Fuchsia* cultivars
  fuchsia
  ✺H:30 in.; S:30 in.; Z:6-10 ●●●●●○

- *Geranium* species and cultivars
  geranium (cranesbill)
  ✺H:20 in.; S:20 in.; Z:4-9 ●●●●○

- *Gerbera jamesonii*
  gerbera daisy
  ✺H:18 in.; S:18 in.; Z:8-11 ●●●●○

- *Hakonechloa macra*
  japanese forest grass
  ✺H:18 in.; S:18 in.; Z:5-9 ●○

- *Helictotrichon sempervirens*
  blue oat grass
  ✺H:30 in.; S:24 in.; Z:4-9 ●

- *Hemerocallis sanguinea* and cultivars
  daylily
  ✺H:24 in.; S:24 in.;Z:3-9 ●●●●●○

- *Heuchera* cultivars
  coral bells
  ✺H:18 in.; S:18 in.; Z:4-8 ●●●●○

- *Hosta* cultivars
  hosta
  ✺H:24 in.; S:36 in.; Z:3-8 ●●○○

- *Iberis sempervirens*
  candytuft
  ✺H:12 in.; S:18 in.; Z:3-9 ○

- *Imperata cylindrica* 'Red Baron'
  japanese blood grass
  ✺H:15 in.; S:24 in.; Z:4-9 ●●

- *Iris* species and cultivars
  iris
  ✺H:18 in.; S:12 in.; Z:3-9 ●●●●●○

- *Lamium maculatum*
  lamium (dead nettle)
  ✺H:12 in.; S:18 in.; Z:3-9 ●●○

- *Leucanthemum* × *superbum*
  shasta daisy
  ✺H:24 in.; S:18 in.; Z:4-9 ○

- *Miscanthus sinensis*
  maiden grass
  ✺H:48 in.; S:36 in.; Z:4-10 ○●

- *Pennisetum setaceum*
  fountain grass
  ✺H:36 in.; S:24 in.; Z:4-9 ●

- *Primula* species and cultivars
  primrose
  ✺H:12 in.; S:10 in.; Z:3-8 ●●●●○

- *Rudbeckia* species and cultivars
  black-eyed susan
  ✺H:24 in.; S:20 in.; Z:3-9 ●○

- *Salvia* species and cultivars
  salvia
  ✺H:18 in.; S:18 in.; Z:4-9 ●●●●○

- *Stachys byzantina*
  lamb's-ear
  ✺H:18 in.; S:18 in.; Z:5-9 ●●●

- *Veronica* species and cultivars
  speedwell
  ✺H:20 in.; S:18 in.; Z:3-9 ●●●●●○

Leucanthemum superbum
shasta daisy

Miscanthus sinensis
maiden grass

Primula species and cultivars
primrose

bulbs

Treat most summer-flowering bulbs, tuberous begonia, dahlia, and gladiolus, as annuals or remove them from the containers in fall and store indoors over winter. Lilies and spring-flowering bulbs survive winter in their pots if you store the pots in an unheated shed or garage to prevent the soil from freezing.

Caladium bicolor
caladium

Canna cultivars
canna

- *Allium* spp.
  allium
  ✳H:12 in.; S:6 in.; Z:4-9 ●●

- *Anemone blanda*
  windflower
  ✸H:6 in.; S:4 in.; Z:4-9 ●●●○

- *Begonia tuberhybrida*
  tuberous begonia
  ✸H:12 in.; S:8 in.; Z:9-11 ●●●●○

- *Caladium bicolor*
  caladium
  ◐H:24 in.; S:20 in.; Z:9-11 ●

- *Canna* cultivars
  canna
  ✳H:30 in.; S:24 in.; Z:8-11 ●●●●○

- *Chionodoxa*
  glory-of-the-snow
  ✸◐H:6 in.; S:3 in.; Z:4-8 ●

- *Crocus* species and cultivars
  crocus
  ✳H:4 in.; S:3 in.; Z:3-8 ●●●●○

- *Dahlia* cultivars
  dahlia
  ✳H:12 in.; S:10 in.; Z:7-11 ●●●●●○

- *Eranthis hyemalis*
  winter aconite
  ✳H:18 in.; S:18 in.; Z:4-8 ●

- *Galanthus nivalis*
  snowdrop
  ✳H:8 in.; S:5 in.; Z:4-8 ○

- *Gladiolus* cultivars
  gladiolus
  ✳H:36 in.; S:12 in.; Z:9-11 ●●●●●○

- *Gladiolus callianthus*
  acidanthera (peacock orchid)
  ✸◐H:24 in.; S:12 in.; Z:7-11 ○

- *Hyacinthus orientalis*
  hyacinth
  ✳H:8 in.; S:6 in.; Z:5-8 ●●●●○

- *Iris reticulata*
  reticulated iris (netted iris)
  ✳H:12 in.; S:3 in.; Z:3-8 ●●

- *Lilium* species and cultivars
  lily
  ✸◐H:36 in.; S:12 in.; Z:3-8 ●●●●○

- *Muscari armeniacum*
  grape hyacinth
  ✳H:8 in.; S:6 in.; Z:3-8 ●●●○

- *Narcissus* species and cultivars
  daffodil
  ✸◐H:12 in.; S:4 in.; Z:3-8 ●●○

- *Tulipa* species and cultivars
  tulip
  ✸◐H:18 in.; S:4 in.; Z:3-8 ●●●●●○

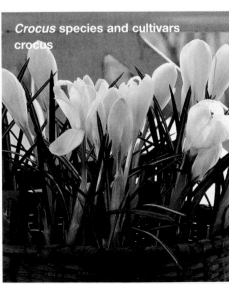
Crocus species and cultivars
crocus

Gladiolus callianthus
acidanthera

Hyacinthus orientalis
hyacinth

key: ✸=sun; ✳=shade; ◐=part sun, part shade H=height; S=spread; Z=zone;
bloom/foliage/fruit colors: ●=yellow; ●=red; ●=orange; ●=purple; ●=lavender; ●=blue; ●=pink; ○=white;
●=variegated; ●=silver/gray

Abutilon species and cultivars
flowering maple

Begonia species and cultivars
angelwing begonia

tropicals

Many of these plants grow into small trees or shrubs in the ground. They grow slightly smaller in pots. Grow one plant per large container for a stunning accent in the garden or on a patio. Bring nonhardy tropicals indoors in fall; set them in a bright sunroom or heated enclosed porch until spring.

- *Abutilon* species and cultivars
  flowering maple
  ✹H:24 in.; S:20 in.; Z:9-11 ●●

- *Alstroemeria* species and cultivars
  pervian lily
  ✹◑H:36 in.; S:24 in.; Z:8-10 ●●○

- *Begonia coccinea* cultivars
  angelwing begonia
  ◑H:36 in.; S:12 in.; Z:9-11 ●●○

- *Bougainvillea* species and cultivars
  bougainvillea
  ✹H:15 ft.; S:4 ft.; Z:9-11 ●●●○

- *Ceratostigma* species and cultivars
  plumbago (leadwort)
  ✹H:6 ft.; S:8 ft.; Z:9-11 ●

- *Clivia miniata*
  clivia (kaffir lily)
  ✹◑H:20 in.; S:18 in.; Z:10-11 ●

- *Datura* species
  datura (angel's trumpet)
  ✹H:30 in.; S:18 in.; Z: 9-11 ●●●

- *Dracaena* species and cultivars
  dracaena
  ◑H:24 in.; S:12 in.; Z: 9-11 ●

- *Eucomis* species
  pineapple lily
  ✹H:18 in.; S:12 in.; Z: 8-11 ○●

- *Guzmania* species
  bromeliad
  ◑H:12 in.; S:10 in.; Z: 10-11 ●●●

- *Kalanchoe* species
  kalanchoe
  ✹◑H:15 in.; S:10 in.; Z: 9-11 ●●●

- *Musa* species
  banana
  ✹H:10 ft.; S:4 ft.; Z: 4-9 ●●

- *Nemesia strumosa* and cultivars
  nemesia
  ✹H:10 in.; S:6 in.; Z: 9-11 ●●●○

- *Phormium* species and cultivars
  phormium (new zealand flax)
  ✹◑H:4 ft.; S:3 ft.; Z: 8-11 ●●●

- *Rhapis excelsa*
  lady palm
  ◑H:5.; S:5.; Z: 8-11

- *Strobilanthes dyeriana*
  persian shield
  ✹H:24 in.; S:18 in.; Z: 10-11 ●●

- *Tibouchina* species
  glory bush
  ✹H:8 ft.; S:6 ft.; Z: 10-11 ●●●

- *Zingiber officinale*
  ginger
  ✹H:36 in.; S:24 in.; Z: 10-11 ●●

Clivia miniata
kaffir lily

Datura species
angel's trumpet

Musa species
banana

vines

Design privacy screens, boundaries around the perimeters of borders, and graceful, flowering accents for patios and decks using annual and perennial vines in planters. Treat vines that are not winter hardy in your area as annuals; all grow quickly enough to make them worth growing in containers.

Ipomoea batatas
sweet potato vine

Mandevilla species and cultivars

- *Anredera cordifolia*
  madeira vine
  ◐◑H:12 ft.; Z:9-11 ○

- *Campsis radicans*
  trumpet vine
  ◐◑H:30 ft.; Z:5-9 ○●●

- *Clematis* species and cultivars
  clematis
  ◐◑H:15 ft.; Z:4-9 ●●●●○

- *Cobaea scandens*
  cup-and-saucer vine
  ◐H:20 ft.; Z:9-11 ●○

- *Gloriosa superba*
  glory lily
  ◐◑H:5 ft.; Z:9-11 ●

- *Hedera* species and cultivars
  ivy
  ◐◑H:30 ft.; Z:5-9 ●●

- *Ipomoea alba*
  moonflower
  ◐H:6 ft.; Z:8-11 ○

- *Ipomoea batatas*
  sweet potato vine
  ◐H:3 ft.; Z:9-11 ●

- *Ipomoea purpurea*
  morning glory
  ◐H:12 ft.; Z:8-11 ●●●●○

- *Jasminum officinale*
  jasmine
  ◐H:20 ft.; Z:7-11 ○

- *Lathyrus latifolius*
  perennial pea
  ◐H:6 ft.; Z:5-9 ●●●○

- *Lonicera* species
  honeysuckle
  ◐H:15 ft.; Z:4-9 ●●

- *Mandevilla* species and cultivars
  mandevilla
  ◐H:15 ft.; Z:10-11 ●●○

- *Passiflora* species
  passionflower
  ◐H:18 in.; Z:5-9 ●●●●●

- *Rosa* cultivars
  climbing rose
  ◐H:10.; Z:3-9 ●●●○

- *Stephanotis floribunda*
  madagascar jasmine
  ◐◑H:8-9 ft.; Z:10-11 ○

- *Thunbergia alata*
  black-eyed susan vine
  ◐H:8 ft.; Z:9-11 ●○

- *Tropaeolum peregrinum*
  canary creeper
  ◐H:8 ft.; Z:9-11 ●

Passiflora species
passionflower

Stephanotis floribunda
madagascar jasmine

Thunbergia alata
black-eyed susan vine

key: ◉=sun; ◉=shade; ◐=part sun, part shade; H=height; S=spread; Z=zone
bloom/foliage/fruit colors: ○=yellow; ●=red; ●=orange; ●=purple; ●=lavender; ●=blue; ●=pink; ○=white;
●=variegated; ●=silver/gray

trailers

Convolvulus species and cultivars
dwarf morning glory

Diascia
twinspur

Plants with lax stems look as good in hanging baskets as those with truly trailing stems. Use them to create a shower of color by hanging the baskets from eaves, pergolas, and overhead porch beams. Set them alone in pots or around the edge of a planter in combination with upright plants in the center.

- *Browallia speciosa*
  browallia
  ❋L:12 in.; Z:9-11 ●

- *Convolvulus tricolor* species and cultivars
  dwarf morning glory
  ❋L:6 ft.; Z:5-9 ●●◐

- *Diascia* species
  twinspur
  ❋◗L:12 in.; Z:8-10 ●

- *Gazania rigens*
  gazania
  ❋L:10 in.; Z:9-10 ○●●

- *Helichrysum petiolatum*
  licorice plant
  ❋L:24 in.; Z:9-11 ●

- *Lobelia erinus* and cultivars
  lobelia
  ❋◗L:12 in.; Z:9-11 ●●●○

- *Lotus berthelotii*
  parrot's beak
  ❋L:24 in.; Z:6-9 ●●●

- *Pelargonium peltatum*
  ivy geranium
  ❋L:24 in.; Z:9-11 ●●●○

- *Plectranthus* cultivars
  swedish ivy
  ◗L:24 in.; Z:9-11 ●○◐

- *Rosmarinus officinalis* 'Prostratus'
  prostrate rosemary
  ❋◗L:18 in.; Z:7-11 ●

- *Sanvitalia procumbens*
  creeping zinnia
  ❋L:15 in..; Z: 9-11 ○●○

- *Scaevola*
  fan flower
  ❋◗L:15 in.; Z:9-11 ●●○

- *Sedum morganium*
  burro's-tail
  ❋◗L:18 in.; Z:9-11 ●

- *Sutera cordata* species and cultivars
  bacopa
  ❋L:10 in.; Z:8-10 ●○

- *Tropaeolum majus*
  nasturtium
  ❋L:5 ft.; Z:9-11 ○●●○

- *Verbena* species and cultivars
  verbena
  ❋L:24 in.; Z:7-10 ●●●○

- *Vinca major* and cultivars
  vinca vine
  ❋◗L:18 in.; Z:4-9 ●●

Lobelia erinus and cultivars
lobelia

Sutera cordata species and cultivars
bacopa

Verbena species and cultivars
verbena

edibles

Select dwarf or patio varieties of vegetable plants, such as tomatoes. Grow vining plants, such as cucumbers and pole beans, up trellises. Plant root vegetables, radishes and carrots, for example, in a container at least 8 to 10 inches deep. In most zones, treat vegetables as annuals.

Capsicum annuum
hot pepper

Fragaria species and cultivars
strawberry

- *Allium* species and cultivars
  onion
  ❁ 9 per 12-in. pot; Z:all ○

- *Beta vulgaris* var. *flavescens*
  swiss chard
  ❁ 4 per 12-in. pot.; Z:all ●

- *Capsicum annuum*
  sweet and hot peppers
  ❁ 1 per 14-in. pot; Z:all ●●●●

- *Cucumis sativus*
  cucumber
  ❁ 1 per 12-in. pot; Z:all ●

- *Cucurbita pepo*
  zucchini
  ❁ 1 per 24-in. pot.; Z:all ●

- *Daucus carota*
  carrot
  ❁ 9 per 12-in. pot; Z:all ●●

- *Dianthus* species and cultivars
  pinks
  ❁ H:18 in.; S:18 in.; Z:4-9 ●●●

- *Eruca sativa*
  arugula
  ❁ 4 per 12-in. pot.; Z:all

- *Fragaria* species and cultivars
  strawberry
  ❁ 5 per 16-in. pot.; Z:6-9 ●○

- *Lactuca sativa* cultivars
  lettuce
  ❁ 4 per 12-in. pot; Z:all ●

- *Lycopersicon* cultivars
  tomato
  ❁ 1 per 18- 24-in. pot; Z:all ●●●●

- *Phaseolus* cultivars
  bush and pole beans
  ❁ 8 per 24-in. pot.; Z:all ●●○

- *Pisum sativum* and cultivars
  peas
  ❁ 8 per 24-in. pot; Z:all

- *Raphanus sativus*
  radish
  ❁ 12 per 12-in. pot; Z:all ●○

- *Solanum melongena*
  eggplant
  ❁ 1 per 24-in. pot; Z:all ●○

- *Spinacia oleracea*
  spinach
  ❁ 4 per 12-in. pot; Z:all

- *Tropaeolum majus*
  nasturtium
  ❁ H:18 in.; S:18 in.; Z:all ●●●

- *Viola odorata*
  sweet violet
  ❁ H:6 in.; S:12 in.; Z:4-9 ●●○

Lycopersicon cultivars
tomato

Solanum melongena
eggplant

Tropaeolum majus
nasturtium

key: ●=sun; ●=shade; ◑=part sun, part shade; H=height; S=spread; Z=zone
bloom/foliage/fruit colors: ●=yellow; ●=red; ●=orange; ●=purple; ●=lavender; ●=blue; ●=pink; ○=white; ●=variegated; ●=silver/gray

Allium schoenoprasum
chives

Cymbopogon citratus
lemongrass

herbs

Pots of herbs beside the kitchen door bring the fragrances, tastes, and colors of an herb garden up close and easy to harvest. In most areas, grow tender perennials, such as bay and rosemary, in containers and bring them indoors when frost threatens in fall. Treat biennials, such as parsley, as annuals.

- *Alchemilla mollis*
  lady's mantle
  ❋◗H:20 in.; S:24 in.; Z:4–8 ●

- *Allium schoenoprasum*
  chives
  ❋◗H:12 in.; S:18 in.; Z:4–9 ●

- *Aloysia triphylla*
  lemon verbena
  ❋H:3 ft.; S:2 ft.; Z:all ●○

- *Anethum graveolens*
  dill
  ❋H:3 ft.; S:1 ft.; Z:all ○

- *Coriandrum sativum*
  cilantro (coriander)
  ❋H:24 in.; S:10 in.; Z:all ●○

- *Cymbopogon citratus*
  lemongrass
  ❋H:36 in.; S:24 in.; Z:all

- *Lavandula* species and cultivars
  lavender
  ❋H:18 in.; S:24 in.; Z:5-9 ●●

- *Melissa officinalis*
  lemon balm
  ❋◗H:24 in.; S:24 in.; Z:4-9 ●

- *Mentha* species and cultivars
  mint
  ❋◗H:24 in.; S:36 in.; Z:4-9 ●

- *Nepeta* x *faassenii*
  catmint
  ❋◗H:24 in.; S:24 in.; Z:4-9 ●●

- *Ocimum basilicum*
  sweet basil
  ❋H:24 in.; S:1 ft.; Z:all ●◗

- *Origanum majorana*
  sweet marjoram
  ❋H:20 in.; S:18 in.; Z:all ○

- *Origanum vulgare*
  oregano
  ❋H:24 in.; S:24 in.; Z:5-9 ●○

- *Petroselinum crispum*
  parsley
  ❋◗H:12 in.; S:12 in.; Z:all

- *Rosmarinus officinalis*
  rosemary
  ❋H:24 in.; S:24 in.; Z:7-10 ●●○

- *Salvia officinalis*
  common sage
  ❋H:24 in.; S:24 in.; Z:4-9 ●●

- *Thymus* species and cultivars
  thyme
  ❋H:12 in.; S:10 in.; Z:4-9 ●

Mentha species and cultivars
peppermint

Ocimum basilicum
basil

Rosmarinus officinalis
rosemary

succulents & alpines

Shallow containers create the perfect home for special plants, such as succulents, cacti, and delicate-looking alpine flowers. Bring tender plants indoors for the winter months.

Armeria maritima cultivars
sea pink

Opuntia microdasys
prickly pear cactus

- *Arabis bryoides*
  rockcress
  ❋H:6 in.; S:12 in.; Z:7-9 ○

- *Armeria maritima* cultivars
  sea pink (thrift)
  ❋H:10 in.; S:8 in.; Z:7-9 ●●○

- *Cereus* species
  orchid cactus
  ❋H:6 ft.; S:10 in.; Z:9-11 ◐●

- *Cyclamen hederifolium*
  dwarf hardy cyclamen
  ❋◐H:5 in.; S:5 in.; Z:6-8 ●○●●

- *Draba* species
  draba
  ❋H:18 in.; S:18 in.; Z:4-8 ○

- *Echeveria* species
  echeveria
  ❋H:5 in.; S:8 in.; Z:8-11 ◐●

- *Graptopetalum paraguayense*
  ghost plant
  ❋H:4 in.; S:10 in.; Z:9-11 ●

- *Haworthia cymbiformis*
  haworthia
  ❋◐H:3 in.; S:6 in.; Z:9-11 ○

- *Iberis sempervirens*
  candytuft
  ❋H:8 in.; S:18 in.; Z:4-9 ○

- *Kalanchoe* species
  kalanchoe
  ❋◐H:24 in.; S:12 in.; Z:9-11 ◐●

- *Mammillaria* species
  pincushion cactus
  ❋H:5 in.; S:2 in.; Z:9-10 ●

- *Opuntia microdasys*
  prickly pear cactus
  ❋H:15 in.; S:6 in.; Z:8-10 ◐●

- *Penstemon hirsutus* 'Pygmaeus'
  penstemon
  ❋H:5 in.; S:5 in.; Z:3-9 ●

- *Portulacaria afra*
  elephant's foot
  ❋H:36 in.; S:24 in.; Z:9-11 ◐●

- *Primula* species
  alpine primrose
  ◐H:6 in.; S:6 in.; Z:7-9 ●●○

- *Saxifraga* species
  saxifrage
  ❋◐H:2 in.; S:5 in.; Z:7-10 ◐○

- *Sedum* species
  sedum
  ❋H:8 in.; S:10 in.; Z:4-11 ○

- *Sempervivum* species and cultivars
  hen and chicks
  ❋H:4 in.; S:18 in.; Z:5-10 ●●○◐

Primula species
alpine primrose

Sedum species
sedum

Sempervivum species and cultivars
hen and chicks

key: ❋=sun; ❋=shade; ◐=part sun, part shade; H=height; S=spread; Z=zone

bloom/foliage/fruit colors: ○=yellow; ●=red; ●=orange; ●=purple; ●=lavender; ●=blue; ●=pink; ○=white; ◐=variegated; ●=silver/gray

Buxus species and cultivars
boxwood

Citrus limon and cultivars
lemon

trees & shrubs

Give most trees and shrubs their own very large containers. Trees suitable for planters grow slowly; even the dwarf forms rarely attain more than a couple of inches of new growth a year.

- *Acer palmatum* var. *dissectum*
  dwarf japanese maple
  ❀◐H:6 ft.; S:6 ft.; Z:6-9 ●

- *Buddleia davidii* cultivars
  dwarf butterfly bush
  ❀●H:30 in.; S:30 in.; Z:5-8 ●●●●○

- *Buxus* species and cultivars
  boxwood
  ❀H:24 in.; S:18 in.; Z:5-9

- *Citrofortunella microcarpa* and cultivars
  calamondin orange
  ❀H:36 in.; S:36 in.; Z:9-11 ●●

- *Citrus limon* and cultivars
  lemon
  ❀H:10 ft.; S:10 ft.; Z:9-11 ●●

- *Daphne* x *burkwoodii*
  daphne
  ❀◐H:36 in.; S:36 in.; Z:4-8 ●●

- *Ilex crenata, I. opaca* cultivars
  dwarf holly
  ❀H:36 in.; S:36 in.; Z:5-9 ●●

- *Juniperus* species and cultivars
  juniper
  ❀◐H:24 in.; S:24 in.; Z:5-9 ●

- *Laurus nobilis*
  bay
  ❀◐H:6 ft.; S:4 ft.; Z:8-10

- *Picea abies* cultivars
  bird's nest spruce
  ❀◐H:6 ft.; S:4 ft.; Z:4-9

- *Pinus thunbergii*
  japanese black pine
  ❀H:36 in.; S:24 in.; Z:4-9

- *Prunus* cultivars
  dwarf cherry
  ❀H:6 ft.; S:5 ft.; Z:4-9 ●○

- *Prunus persica* cultivars
  dwarf peach
  ❀H:4 ft.; S:4 ft.; Z:5-8 ●○

- *Prunus* x *domestica* cultivars
  plum
  ❀H:8 ft.; S:8 ft.; Z:5-8 ○

- *Rhododendron* species and cultivars
  azalea (rhododendron)
  ◐H:24 in.; S:24 in.; Z:6-8 ●○

- *Rosa* cultivars
  rose
  ❀H:18 in.; S:18 in.; Z:4-9 ●●●●●

- *Taxus* cultivars
  yew
  ❀◐H:24 in.; S:24 in.; Z:6-9

Laurus nobilis
bay

Prunus x domestica cultivars
plum

Rosa cultivars
rose

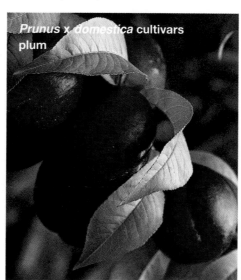

sources

Mail–Order Nurseries and Garden Suppliers

Brent and Becky's Bulbs (B) free
7463 Heath Trail
Gloucester, VA 23061
877/661-2852
www.brentandbeckysbulbs.com

Burpee (S) free
300 Park Ave.
Warminster, PA 18991–0001
800/333-5808
www.burpee.com

The Cook's Garden (S) free
P.O. Box 5010
Hodges, SC 29653-5010
800/457-9703
www.cooksgarden.com

Etera (P) $7.00
14113 River Bend Rd.
Mount Vernon, WA 98273
800/753-8372
www.etera.com

Forestfarm (P, T) $5.00
990 Tetherow Rd.
Williams, OR 97544-9599
541/846-7269
www.forestfarm.com

Gardener's Supply Co. (H, C) free
128 Intervale Rd.
Burlington, VT 05401
888/833-1412
www.gardeners.com

Heronswood Nursery Ltd. (P, T) $5.00
7530 N.E. 288th St.
Kingston, WA 98346-9502
360/297-4172
www.heronswood.com

Jackson & Perkins Co. (B, P, R, H) free
One Rose Lane
Medford, OR 97501
877/456-8800
www.jacksonandperkins.com

Kinsman Co., Inc. (H, C) free
P.O. Box 428
Point Pleasant, PA 18950-0357
800/733-4146
www.kinsmangarden.com

Miller Nurseries (F, P, T) free
5080 W. Lake Rd.
Canandaigua, NY 14424-8904
800/836-9630
www.millernurseries.com

Nor'East Miniature Roses (R) free
P.O. Box 307
Rowley, MA 01969
800/426-6485
www.noreast-miniroses.com

Park Seed (B, P, R, S, T) free
One Parkton Ave.
Greenwood, SC 29649-0001
800/213-0076
www.parkseed.com

Peaceful Valley Farm Supply
(F, S, T, H) free
P.O. Box 2209
Grass Valley, CA 95945
888/784-1722
www.groworganic.com

Shepherd's Garden Seeds
(B, P, R, S, T) free
30 Irene St.
Torrington, CT 06790-6658
860/482-3638
www.shepherdseeds.com

Stokes Tropicals (P) $7.95
P.O. Box 9868
New Iberia, LA 70562
800/624-9706
www.stokestropicals.com

Thompson & Morgan Inc. (S) $2.25
P.O. Box 1308
Jackson, NJ 08527-0308
800/274-7333
www.thompson-morgan.com

Wayside Gardens (B, P, R, T) free
One Garden Lane
Hodges, SC 29695-0001
888/817-1124
www.waysidegardens.com

White Flower Farm (B, P, T, H) free
P.O. Box 50
Litchfield, CT 06759-0050
800/503-9624
www.whiteflowerfarm.com

This map of climate zones helps you select plants for your garden that will survive a typical winter in your region. The United States Department of Agriculture (USDA) developed the map, basing the zones on the lowest recorded temperatures across the country. Numbered 1 to 11, Zone 1 is the coldest area and Zone 11 is the warmest.

Plants are classified by the coldest temperature and zone they can endure. For example, plants hardy to Zone 6 survive where winter temperatures drop to −10° F. Those hardy to Zone 8 die long before it's that cold. These plants may grow in colder regions but must be replaced each year. Plants rated for a range of Hardiness Zones can usually survive winter in the coldest region as well as tolerate the summer heat of the warmest one.

To find your Hardiness Zone, note the approximate location of your community on the map, then match the color band marking that area to the key.

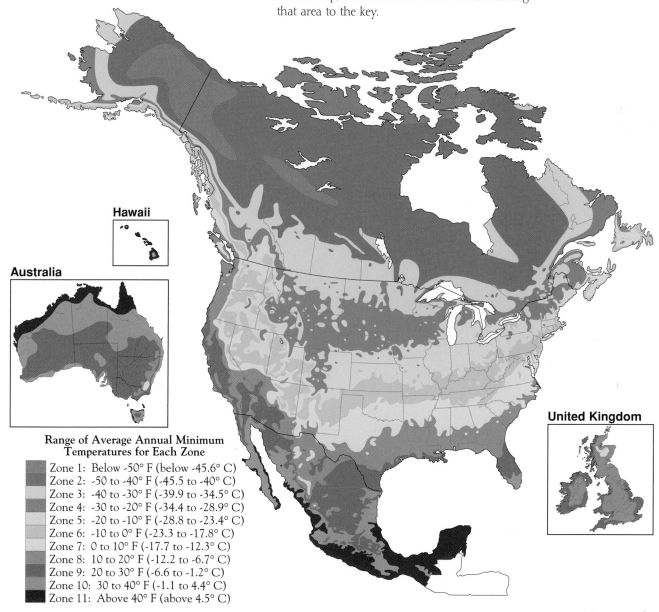

Hawaii

Australia

United Kingdom

Range of Average Annual Minimum Temperatures for Each Zone

Zone 1: Below -50° F (below -45.6° C)
Zone 2: -50 to -40° F (-45.5 to -40° C)
Zone 3: -40 to -30° F (-39.9 to -34.5° C)
Zone 4: -30 to -20° F (-34.4 to -28.9° C)
Zone 5: -20 to -10° F (-28.8 to -23.4° C)
Zone 6: -10 to 0° F (-23.3 to -17.8° C)
Zone 7: 0 to 10° F (-17.7 to -12.3° C)
Zone 8: 10 to 20° F (-12.2 to -6.7° C)
Zone 9: 20 to 30° F (-6.6 to -1.2° C)
Zone 10: 30 to 40° F (-1.1 to 4.4° C)
Zone 11: Above 40° F (above 4.5° C)

index

index

index

photo credits

David Cavagnaro
24

Ros Creasy
9 (top) 10 (top)
23 (bottom) 26 (center) 27 (top)
27 (bottom left) 36 (right)
37 (top left) 37 (top right)
37 (bottom left) 40 (top left)
40 (top right) 40 (bottom right)
41 (top) 41 (bottom right) 49 (top)
65 (top right) 65 (left)
86 (bottom left) 87 (left)
93 (bottom right) 111 (bottom left)

114 (bottom right)
122 (bottom left) 125 (bottom right)
126 botton right)
127 (bottom left) 131 (bottom left)
132 (bottom center) 133 (bottom left)

Saxon Holt
18 (top right)
41 (bottom left) 66 (top left)

Dency Kane
23 (bottom right)
100 (bottom) 102 (bottom left)
110 (bottom)

Rosemary Kautzky
111 (top left) 112 (bottom right)
113 (left) 115 (bottom left)
124 (bottom left) 125 (top center)
129 (bottom right) 132 (top center)

Charles Mann
26 (bottom left) 101 (right)
122 (top center) 125 (bottom center)
129 (top center) 132 (top center)

metric conversions

US Units to Metric Equivalents

to convert from	multiply by	to get
Inches	25.400	Millimetres
Inches	2.540	Centimetres
Feet	30.480	Centimetres
Feet	0.3048	Metres
Yards	0.9144	Metres
Square inches	6.4516	Square centimetres
Square feet	0.0929	Square metres
Square yards	0.8361	Square metres
Acres	0.4047	Hectares
Cubic inches	16.387	Cubic centimetres
Cubic feet	0.0283	Cubic metres
Cubic feet	28.316	Litres
Cubic yards	0.7646	Cubic metres
Cubic yards	764.550	Litres

To convert from degrees Celsius to degrees Fahrenheit, multiply by ⁹⁄₅, then add 32.

Metric Units to US Equivalents

to convert from	multiply by	to get
Millimetres	0.0394	Inches
Centimetres	0.3937	Inches
Centimetres	0.0328	Feet
Metres	3.2808	Feet
Metres	1.0936	Yards
Square centimetres	0.1550	Square inches
Square metres	10.764	Square feet
Square metres	1.1960	Square metres
Hectares	2.4711	Acres
Cubic centimetres	0.0610	Cubic inches
Cubic metres	35.315	Cubic feet
Litres	0.0353	Cubic feet
Cubic metres	1.308	Cubic yards
Litres	0.0013	Cubic yards

To convert from degrees Fahrenheit (F) to degrees Celsius (C), first subtract 32, then multiply by ⁵⁄₉.